COLORADO

OUTDOOR ACTIVITY GUIDE

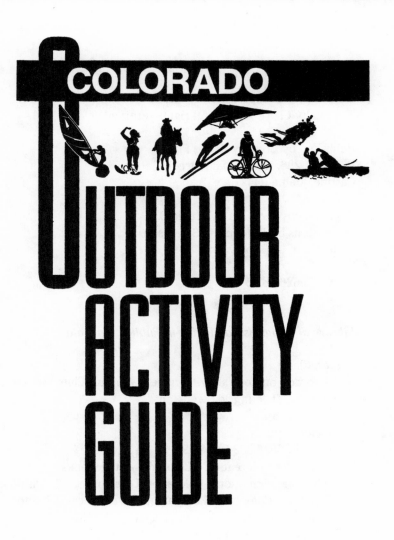

COLORADO

OUTDOOR ACTIVITY GUIDE

Claire Walter

Illustrated by Dale Ingrid Swensson

Country Roads Press

C A S T I N E • M A I N E

Colorado Outdoor Activity Guide
© 1995 by Claire Walter. All rights reserved.

Published by Country Roads Press
P.O. Box 286, Lower Main Street
Castine, Maine 04421

Text and cover design by Studio 3.
Illustrations by Dale Ingrid Swensson.
Typesetting by Typeworks.

ISBN 1-56626-082-5

Library of Congress Cataloging-in-Publication Data

Walter, Claire
    Colorado outdoor activity guide / author, Claire Walter ;
illustrator, Dale Ingrid Swensson.
        p.   cm.
    Includes index.
    ISBN 1-56626-082-5 : $9.95
        1. Outdoor recreation—Colorado—Guidebooks.
    2. Outdoor recreation—Colorado—Directories.   3. Outdoor
recreation—Colorado—Equipment and supplies—Directories.
    4. Colorado—Description and travel.   I. Title.
    GV191.42.C6W35   1995
    796.5'09788—dc20   94-46636
                                                              CIP

Printed in the United States of America.
10 9 8 7 6 5 4 3 2 1

To Ruth Rejnis,
a former neighbor, a good friend,
a fine writer, but, alas,
still a dedicated flatlander

CONTENTS

INTRODUCTION

Located close to the geographical center of the continental United States, Colorado is also close to the hearts of lovers of the outdoors. It's the state where mountains soar, rivers roil, fish strike, snow falls in a feather-light blanket, and a cerulean sky turns every scene into one of postcard beauty. Hikers, skiers, campers, anglers, balloonists, climbers, kayakers, horseback riders, and enthusiasts of a myriad of other activities choose to live or vacation in Colorado for this abundance of outdoor options and the matchless environment for outdoor adventures from mild to wild—on the ground, over the snow, in the water, in the air.

For the outdoor adventurer, Colorado offers more than a thousand square miles of wilderness, some 65,000 miles of streams and rivers, and 2,000 fishable lakes and reservoirs that yield over two million fish a year. There is also an abundance of campgrounds, hiking paths, bike paths, and four-wheel-drive roads. To many people, Colorado and skiing are synonymous. The state's twenty-six downhill ski areas annually tally more than eleven million skier visits, each representing one skier or snowboarder on the slopes for one day. Although Colorado's population has yet to reach four million, roughly 20 percent of all skier visits recorded in the United States take place here.

Still, Colorado's soul is not statistical, and numbers are not what the state is about. They merely quantify the state's recreational riches. Katherine Lee Bates was in Colorado Springs when she penned the words to "America the Beautiful." What she saw as she gazed toward Pikes Peak was "purple mountain majesties across the fruited plain," and those words, etched into America's collective consciousness, define Colorado to this day.

Bates and countless other crafters of prose and poetry have described Colorado's wonders with suitable eloquence, but this book isn't meant to parade more effusive adjectives before you. Nor is it a memoir of trails I've hiked, slopes I've skied, mountains I've climbed, rivers I've rafted, horses I've ridden, streams I've fished, or any of the other excellent adventures that constitute research for such a book. It is a resource to you in your pursuit of outdoor pleasures. Almost every activity is available in Colorado (there's plenty of boating on lakes and reservoirs and even scuba diving beneath the surface), but I've chosen to focus on those that the state's majestic mountains, high valleys, and shimmering rivers render special. Therefore, I've included hiking, climbing, horseback riding, four-wheel driving, whitewater rafting, backcountry skiing, downhill skiing, and fly-fishing. Though the state offers fine golf, tennis, motorboating, windsurfing, sailing, waterskiing, and in-line skating, I've not put these in because the mountains are not the key to their enjoyment. I've left out hunting because of my own distaste for it.

In 1993, as a result of a controversial budget-limiting constitutional amendment, the Colorado Tourism Board closed. Since this clearinghouse for information about all of Colorado's myriad wonders does not exist at this writing, it is now necessary to tap into many sources. This book, therefore, is an attempt to fill the information gap, as well as to provide an overview of, and, I hope, some insight into, Colorado's offerings. It is filled with addresses and numbers (current as of late 1994) that you'll need to plan your own outdoor adventures—not a how-to but a where-to book. To describe the mountains and plains, the lakes and rivers, the forests and deserts in all their glory would fill volumes, so I've opted instead to present what these natural playgrounds offer to the active traveler or resident—a wide-ranging guide to what you can do outdoors in Colorado.

ORIENTATION

Colorado, a 104,247-square-mile rectangle, is geographically divided into three zones. Gently rolling plains reminiscent of Kansas or Nebraska extend across the eastern portion of the state. The towering peaks that distinguish the center and some of the west rival the world's great mountain ranges and have become symbols of the state's scenic splendor. It is there that most of Colorado's abundant outdoor activities are concentrated. The magical mesa country that characterizes the rest of western Colorado is composed of canyons and plateaus, akin to the arid Southwestern states.

Colorado is America's highest state, with five times the mountain area of Switzerland, and a thousand mountains that have summits two miles or more above sea level (fifty-four of them topping 14,000 feet and collectively nicknamed "fourteeners"). Most of this mountain area—23.5 million acres—is controlled public land in the form of

1

national parks, national forests, state and county land, and even mountain parks under the protection of major cities. More than 612,000 acres—nearly a thousand square miles— have been declared wilderness, forever protected from mining, logging, road building, dam construction, campgrounds, visitors centers, or other intrusions, with an additional 154,000 acres under similar but less stringent restrictions.

Much of the remaining backcountry has been designated as multi-use land, where controlled logging, mining, grazing, and other enterprises are permitted by the U.S. Forest Service (USFS) and the Bureau of Land Management (BLM). Along with extractive uses, these lands, which belong to us all, offer rafting, hiking, horsepacking, camping, fishing, and skiing. Recreational opportunities there are rarely matched and nowhere surpassed for quality and quantity, with options ranging from highly developed ski resorts, dude ranches, and slickly run commercial enterprises to backcountry expeditions that offer equal measures of scenery and solitude. The USFS and the BLM are becoming increasingly responsive to the needs and wants of these widely varied recreational users.

THE LAY OF THE LAND

THE MOUNTAINS

The highest of the 2,000-mile-long Rocky Mountains are concentrated in central and western Colorado. The Continental Divide winds through the state, with its easternmost protuberance in northern Colorado. The mountains between the eastern Plains and the Continental Divide are known as the Front Range. They are the most accessible to the big Denver–Boulder–Fort Collins population center. They extend south to the Rampart Range and the Wet Mountains.

Proceeding westward and scanning from north to south, the next group is collectively known as the Central Rockies. It includes the Park Range, Gore Range, Tenmile Range, Mosquito Range, and Sangre de Cristo Range. The Arkansas River separates the Tenmile/Mosquito groups from the Sawatch Range, which contains Colorado's highest summits.

In contrast to the preceding ranges, which run primarily north-south, the Elk Mountains, the West Elk Mountains, Colorado's Central Rockies, the La Garita Mountains, and the Cochetopa Hills just to the south run essentially east-west. In the western part of the state, the topography has plateau, mesa and canyon, and mountainous segments. The Uncompahgre Plateau, the San Miguels, the La Plata Mountains, and the San Juan Mountains angle across the southwestern corner of the state, jutting like a juggernaut into the arid western section. Grand Mesa, just east of Grand Junction, is the world's largest flattop mountain, but not to be confused with the Flat Top Range, the most northwestwardly group in the state.

LIFE ZONES

The difference in altitude between Colorado's highest and lowest points, respectively Mount Elbert and the Arkansas River Valley at the Kansas border, is more than 10,000 feet. The great elevations between the plains and peaks enable hikers to pass through as many life zones as they would

3

on a land journey of hundreds of miles. Every 1,000 vertical feet is equivalent to roughly 500 north-south miles. The plant communities, representing about 4,500 species, vary by rainfall, temperature, and elevation. The mountains eloquently reveal how elevation influences living things.

Life Zone, Description, Elevation Range, Plants

Foothill or Transition
Foothills
6,000–8,000 feet
Ponderosa pine, oak, juniper, aspen

Montane or Canadian
Lower mountains
8,000–10,000 feet
Lodgepole pine, Douglas fir, ponderosa pine, blue spruce, limber pine, white fir

Sub-Alpine or Hudsonian
Higher mountains to timberline
10,000–11,500 feet
Limber pine, Engelmann spruce, ponderosa pine, sub-alpine fir (often shaped into "flag trees" by the prevailing winds)

Alpine or Arctic
Above timberline
Above 11,500 feet
Dwarf willow, grasses, sedges, tundra flowers, lichen

During the short, intense growing season in the high country, Colorado is one of nature's finest gardens. The wildflower season starts with the pasqueflowers of the foothills early in spring and the avalanche lilies that follow receding snowfields. It continues with the mountain harebell, whose drooping blue bells poke up between the rocks well until fall. A hike will reveal clusters of flowers beside rushing mountain streams, fields of multi-colored blossoms in nature's own rock garden, and tiny tundra plants thriving in the harsh climate above the tree line. The state flower of Colorado is the columbine, and the blue-and-white variety is found in forest clearings, mountain meadows, and even rock fields through much of the flower season.

Wildflower season progresses with elevation, and the abundant wildflowers of late spring and early summer are reason enough for a mountain hike at one altitude or another during the warm months. Spring comes early to the meadows and south-facing woodlands of the foothill zone, where flowers peak in late May and early June.

Low meadows may be dry by July, when the montane zone shows splendid color. July is the peak season for wildflowers in much of the mountain area, and midmonth is when Crested Butte puts on its sensational Wildflower Festival, even as the meadows become warm and dry and the best flowers may be in the woodlands. Streams run fast from melt-off in the high snowfields of the sub-Alpine and Alpine zones throughout July, with fine flower displays at the highest elevations into August.

By Labor Day, the feeling of autumn permeates the Rockies, and by late September or early October the golden display of changing aspens is the season's last spectacular show before winter.

5

WILDLIFE

Some 960 animal species live in Colorado, in habitats from short-grass prairie to tundra, so a hike with binoculars or long-lens camera usually results in some rewarding sightings. Many animals migrate among life zones, spending summers at high elevations, staying away from heavily trafficked areas, and returning to lower elevations in fall. Occasionally, a moose can be spotted wading in a lowland marsh, and bighorn sheep (the Colorado state animal) and mountain goats inhabit the high country.

Deer, elk, and antelope are the most common large animals, and the best times to see them are dawn and sunset. At higher elevations, expect to see pikas, marmots, and perhaps ptarmigan. Chipmunks thrive in various life zones throughout hiking season, so at the very least, you'll surely see these endearing little rodents.

Airborne wildlife includes birds from peregrines and golden eagles to hummingbirds, and numerous butterfly species. Sometimes, you'll spot something that's not exotic at all but astonishes nonetheless—perhaps a colony of ladybugs two miles above sea level.

The Colorado Division of Wildlife, which aggressively promotes wildlife viewing through its Watchable Wildlife program, publishes guides on what to look for and how to recognize what you're looking at. *Watching Wildlife Close to Home: Colorado Mountain Region* and *Bighorn Sheep Watching Guide* are available through the division and at bookstores. The agency also maintains a Watchable Wildlife Hotline, 303-291-7416.

Colorado Division of Wildlife
6060 Broadway
Denver, CO 80216
303-297-1192

THE RIVERS

One of the state's several nicknames is "mother of rivers," because it is home to the headwaters of the Colorado, Arkansas, and Rio Grande Rivers. They start as trickles in the high country, but it's not long before small streams become powerful rivers, carving deep gorges through the rock. Inevitably, Colorado's canyons are compared with the Grand Canyon, and they measure up well for rafting— partly because of the beauty and variety, partly because many sections are suitable for short trips, and partly because there are so many rivers and outfitters that you can usually book a river trip even on relatively short notice. Rafting the Grand Canyon may be exciting, but rafting is also spectacular in the Black Canyon of the Gunnison, Ruby Canyon of the Colorado, Lodore Canyon of the Green River, and Royal Gorge of the Arkansas. Seeing the land from the water provides a different perspective, a geology lesson come to life. Between the roaring whitewaters are tranquil stretches that provide opportunities to relax and watch the passing scenery.

The Colorado River is noteworthy because of the incredible canyons it has carved (including the Grand Canyon three states away in Arizona) and because it gave its name to the state. It starts on the west side of Rocky

Mountain National Park, feeds into and flows out of Grand Lake, which is the state's largest natural lake, and continues southwest to the Utah border. Eventually, it dribbles into the sand at the tip of the Sea of Cortez (or Gulf of California).

At 1,887 miles, the Rio Grande is the second longest river in the country. Its headwaters are north of the town of South Fork on the east side of Wolf Creek Pass, and it flows south into New Mexico and eventually forms the Texas-Mexico border. Its most impressive sections are not in Colorado, but its in-state merits are not lost on legions of wildlife enthusiasts, canoeists, rafters, and, most of all, anglers.

The Arkansas gets its start north of Leadville, quickly broadening and deepening to become the most frequently rafted, canoed, and kayaked river in the nation. It passes south with numerous stunning fourteeners on its distant right bank and then curves east, meeting the plains in Pueblo, and eventually flowing across the Kansas border at the lowest elevation in America's highest state.

THE SKIING

Much of the best skiing in North America is found in Colorado. The state's five most distinctive ski-resort towns—Aspen, Breckenridge, Steamboat, Telluride, and Vail—are world-class resorts by anyone's measure, with expansive ski terrain and exceptional on-mountain facilities and services. Their ski slopes are accessible by the most modern lifts and are covered in a combination of cloud-light powder and machine-made snow, all manicured to be skier-friendly.

They set the standard for on-mountain services, but the snow is just as good on mountains whose names are not household words. Eldora and Loveland are each about an hour from metro Denver. Winter Park is a sprawling multi-mountain complex just west of the Continental Divide that consistently ranks high in the popularity polls among knowledgeable locals. Copper Mountain, Keystone, and Snowmass each have skiing on several peaks and lodging in new developments at the base. SilverCreek is a small, self-contained resort that's the perfect place to learn how to ski. Beaver Creek is luxurious skiing for the carriage trade. Cuchara Valley, Powderhorn, Purgatory, and Ski Sunlight are casual, laid-back ski areas. Arapahoe Basin, Monarch, Ski Cooper, and Wolf Creek are old-style ski areas, pure and simple, that are located so high on mountain passes that they require no snowmaking backup at all.

SEARCH-AND-RESCUE FUNDING

Colorado's high country is unsurpassed in its beauty, and it is also known for the unpredictability of its weather and the perils that altitude, avalanches, and unanticipated storms can inflict on the outdoor enthusiast. Traditionally, rural sheriff's departments and search-and-rescue organizations, many of them staffed by volunteers, have been called upon to look for the injured, the unprepared, and the simply unlucky who become lost in the backcountry. Each chapter of this book contains some basic cautions for those who participate in outdoor activities, but even experienced backcountry users are sometimes injured or caught. Taxpayers in rural counties have been picking up much of the tab for these search-and-rescue operations. Although these costs have long been supplemented by fees paid by hunters, anglers, snowmobilers, and off-road vehicle owners, county commissioners, assaulted by the tidal wave of cutting government costs at all levels, have been pressured to cut subsidized search-and-rescue operations and begin charging people who are rescued. In 1995, a voluntary $1.00 certificate was made available to hikers, backcountry skiers and snowshoers, snowmobilers, climbers, and wildlife watchers in order to continue making gratis searches possible. It seems to be a small enough price to pay to support the efforts that we hope we will never need. Certificates are available from the Colorado Division of Wildlife (see Appendix) or through stores and outfitters that sell hunting and fishing licenses.

2 HORSEPOWER

Sightseeing from a saddle is sensational in Colorado. Trail riding is perfect for anyone who wants to look at Colorado's unsurpassed scenery instead of down at the trail; for children, who tire easily; or for those who are not in shape or not interested in mountain hiking. It's easier to cover distances on a horse than on foot, and easier too for overnight trips, because the equines lug both the supplies and the people. However, if you like to hike but want animal aid to bear the burden, another option is llama trekking, an activity that's becoming more popular in the Rocky Mountains.

Beyond the practical aspects of exploring the backcountry with a horse, there's the mystique of riding. The world looks different from atop a horse, and the world looks at the rider differently, too. Nothing so symbolizes the West as a horse and rider moving as one across the plains, fording a stream, or climbing a narrow trail clinging to a mountainside. Colorado provides ample opportunities to live the fantasy—much as Billy Crystal and his pals did in the movie *City Slickers*. In fact, the commercial cattle-drive business is booming, providing everyone with the opportunity to experience life on the trail, complete with thundering hooves and chuck-wagon meals.

For general information on riding and the Colorado horse scene, contact:

Colorado Horsemen's Council
P.O. Box 1125
Arvada, CO 80001
303-279-4546

RIDING ON FEDERAL LANDS

Whether you have your own horse or lease one, Colorado's wide-open spaces and scenic forests provide a peerless playground for experienced riders. There are restrictions on where horses are permitted, but with so much land, you won't soon run out of places to ride. In general, horses are allowed on most Bureau of Land Management (BLM) roads and trails, on many national forest roads, and on selected trails in national park and wilderness areas. With its involvement in managing a great deal of ranching land, it is natural that the BLM also permits horses on the open range. Designated horse campsites have been established in many public land areas, which is important for anyone planning a pack trip. No matter where you take them, animals must be tethered away from lakes and water sources. Contact the appropriate government agency, listed in the Appendix, for information on trails and open range where you may ride.

12

TRAIL RIDES

Outfitters offer itineraries of all lengths and all sorts, from short rides where a meal may be the reward to multi-day pack trips (including backcountry camping) where being away from it all is the goal and camp dinners are just part of the experience. Trips fit into various style categories, from gourmet safaris that happen to be in the backcountry to bare-bones outdoor adventures that happen to include horses. The animals come in various sizes and temperaments, and outfitters aim to have a match for all riders from novices to skilled equestrians. Telluride Horseback Adventures' advertising flyer puts it whimsically and succinctly:

"Gentle horses for gentle people.

Fast horses for fast people.

And, for people who don't like to ride,

Horses that don't like to be rode!"

Trail rides may be as short as an hour or as long as a full day. Common formats are breakfast rides, dinner rides, and all-day horse trips including lunch. Steak-fry rides, sunset rides, and dinner rides are also popular. Some operators offer pony rides for small children and even have petting zoos. While there are numerous equestrian centers and even hunt clubs where English riding is practiced, Colorado is essentially a Western-saddle state. A simple trail ride with an outfitter requires no instruction or experience, but those with more ambition can take riding lessons, and those with none at all may prefer a hayride. Many stables and outfitters will rent horses to experienced riders who prefer to go out on their own. Most outfitters also organize overnight pack trips for fishing or just exploring the backcountry. Some operations are seasonal, others are year-round, and those that are near established resorts frequently offer shuttle service to the barn.

OUTFITTERS, RIDES, AND OTHER DETAILS

A & A Historical Trails
P.O. Box 374
2380 Riverside
Idaho Springs, CO 80452
970-567-4808
One- to eight-hour rides on old mining roads; cookout rides; moonlight rides over the mountains to the historic mining boomtown turned modern-day gambling boomtown of Central City

All Seasons Ranch
P.O. Box 252
Craig, CO 81626
970-879-2606, 970-284-4526
Walton Creek Canyon fishing rides; family trail rides; wilderness pack trips; Routt National Forest

Aspen Wilderness Outfitters
320 West Main Street
Aspen, CO 81611
970-920-3839
White River National Forest luxury pack and naturalist trips with 10,2000-foot base camp; Hunter Creek Wilderness morning trail rides

A. J. Brink Outfitters
3406 Sweetwater Road

Gypsum, CO 81637
970-524-9301
Steak-fry rides to the Flat Tops Wilderness; various picnic rides; winter rides; also Maroon Bells–Snowmass and Rawhah

Big Mountain Outfitters
P.O. Box 1947
Rifle, CO 81650
970-625-2222
Trail rides on 10,000 private acres; plus access to BLM and national forest trails

Brown's Canyon Horse Leasing
P.O. Box 123
Salida, CO 81201
719-395-2361, 719-395-2447
Chalf Creek; one-hour to half-day rides

Brush Creek Outfitters
P.O. Box 5621
Snowmass Village, CO 81615
970-923-4252
One-hour through full-day rides; breakfast and dinner rides

Buena Vista Family Campground
Riding Stables
27700 County Road 303
Buena Vista, CO 81211
800-621-9960, 719-395-8318
Half- and full-day and sunset rides; Midland Hill and Trout Creek

C & M Outfitters
P.O. Box 277
Fairplay, CO 80440
719-836-3388
Buffalo Peaks and Midland area

Canyon Creek Outfitters
P.O. Box 862
Glenwood Springs, CO 81602
970-984-2000, 970-984-2052
Two-hour to all-day rides; sunset steak-supper ride; Saddle and Paddle combo of riding and rafting; White River National Forest and Holy Cross Wilderness

Capitol Peak Outfitters
9554 State Highway 82
Carbondale, CO 81263
970-963-0211
Maroon Lake, Capitol Lake, Williams Lake, Thomas Lake, Buttermilk Meadows, Aspen to Crested Butte rides

Collegiate Peaks Outfitters
P.O. Box 973
Buena Vista, CO 8121
719-395-8085,
719-395-4000 (stable)
San Isabel National Forest; Collegiate Peaks area; breakfast and steak rides

Cowpoke Corner Corral
P.O. Box 2214
Estes Park, CO 80517
970-586-5890

Rocky Mountain National Park and Roosevelt National Forest; breakfast and dinner rides

Crazy Horse Camping Resort
Riding Stables
33975 U.S. 24 North
Buena Vista, CO 81211
800-888-7320, 719-395-2323
Clear Creek; fourteeners areas

Del's Triangle 3 Ranch
P.O. Box 333
Clark, CO 80428
970-879-3495
Routt National Forest; Mt. Zirkel Wilderness; winter rides

Eagles Nest Equestrian Center
P.O. Box 495
Silverthorne, CO 80498
970-468-0677
Arapaho National Forest; breakfast, lunch, and dinner rides

Elk River Guest Ranch
29840 County Road 64
Clark, CO 80428
800-750-6220, 970-879-6220
Routt National Forest rides; steak-dinner rides

Fantasy Ranch
P.O. Box 236
Crested Butte, CO 81224
970-349-5425

Crested Butte Mountain; Crested Butte to Aspen rides; winter rides a specialty

4 Eagle Ranch
4098 State Highway 131
Wolcott, CO 81655
970-926-3372 (information),
970-926-1234 (tack room)
595-acre ranch; winter rides available

Harvard City Stables
See Collegiate Peaks Outfitters, above

Hi Country Stables
3100 Airport Road
Boulder, CO 80301
Glacier Creek Stables: 970-586-3244
Moraine Park Stables: 970-586-2327
Rocky Mountain National Park rides. From Moraine Park: Beaver Meadows, Deer Mountain, Cub Lake, Mill Creek, Ute Indian Trail. From Glacier Creek: Bierstadt Lake, Wind River Trail, Beaver Lake, Mill Creek, Bear Lake

High Meadows Ranch
P.O. Box 771216
Steamboat Springs, CO 80477
800-457-4453, 970-736-8416
Routt National Forest

Hyatt Guides and Outfitters
P.O. Box 1288
Montrose, CO 81402
303-249-9733, 303-249-6389

Two-hour and half- and full-day rides in Uncompahgre National Forest

Indian Peaks Outfitters
23567 State Highway 119
Nederland, CO 80466
303-258-0567,
303-581-0567 (metro Denver)
Half- and full-day trips; Roosevelt National Forest

Keystone Resort
P.O. Box 38
Keystone, CO 80435
800-222-0188, 970-468-2316
Arapaho National Forest; Snake River; breakfast rides

Lazy F Bar Outfitters
P.O. Box 383
Gunnison, CO 81230
970-349-7593, 970-641-0193
Crested Butte Mountain, Brush Creek and East River Valleys, Ferris Creek, Strand Hill, Cement Creek

Mt. Princeton Riding Stable
See Brown's Canyon Horse Leasing, above

Over the Hill Outfitters
3624 County Road 203
Durango, CO 81301
970-247-9289 (year-round),
970-259-2834 (summer)
San Juan National Forest; breakfast and supper rides; family pack trips

Pa and Ma's
Breakfast- and lunch-ride reservations are
taken by the Leadville Chamber of Commerce
719-486-3900
"We have no phone," say Carroll (Pa) and Kathie (Ma) Johnson, "so come and see us." Their ranch is located four miles west of Leadville off U.S. 24; turn right on East Tennessee Road. Breakfast and lunch rides; short trail rides

Peak to Peak Adventure Center
Colorado State Highway 119
Nederland, CO 80466
303-258-3426
Roosevelt National Forest; brunch and sunset dinner rides

Snowmass Falls Outfitters
P.O. Box 686
Carbondale, CO 81623
970-923-6343
West Snowmass Creek Primitive Area; Maroon Bells–Snowmass Wilderness

Snowmass Stables
P.O. Box 608
Snowmass Village, CO 81615
970-923-3075
Breakfast, lunch, and dinner rides; Burnt Mountain and Wildcat Ridge

Solomon Creek Outfitters
P.O. Box 767
Oak Creek, CO 80467

970-736-8239, 970-736-2483
Routt National Forest; specializes in pack trips for wildlife
viewing and photography

Sombrero Ranches
3300 Airport Road, Box A
Boulder, CO 80301
Office: 303-442-0258
Estes Park Ranch: 970-586-4577
Grand Lake Ranch: 970-627-3514
Roosevelt-Arapaho National Forest; Rocky Mountain
National Park; breakfast and steak-dinner rides

Steamboat Lake Outfitters
P.O. Box 749
Clark, CO 80428
800-342-1889, 970-879-4404, 970-879-5590
Steamboat Lake; Mt. Zirkel Wilderness

Steamboat Stable
P.O. Box 770885
Steamboat Springs, CO 80477
970-879-2306
Trail, breakfast, and dinner rides; pack trips; Routt National
Forest

Sundance Adventure Center
3371 Gold Lake Road
Ward, CO 80481
303-499-4940
Half- and full-day and dinner rides around Ward and
Nederland

Sunset Ranch
P.O. Box 770/876
Steamboat Springs, CO 80477
970-879-0954
Yampa Valley, Routt National Forest

T Lazy 7 Ranch
P.O. Box 240
Maroon Creek Road
Aspen, CO 81612
970-925-7254
Breakfast, lunch, and dinner rides; Maroon Bells rides

Telluride Horseback Adventures
c/o Telluride Sports
P.O. Box 1140
Telluride, CO 81435
800-828-7547, 970-728-4477 (Telluride Sports),
970-728-9611 (barn)
San Juan National Forest; rides to Alta ghost town and Mill Creek Basin; one- and two-hour rides; breakfast and dinner rides; "Ride with Roudy," Telluride wrangler featured in national TV commercials

Tiger Run Tours
P.O. Box 1418
Breckenridge, CO 80424
970-453-2231, 970-623-3032 (Denver)
Short rides in Dry Gulch

Trail Skills
Lost Trail Ranch

Highway Contract No. 70, Box 7
Creede, CO 81139
970-852-5194
Family-oriented multi-day trips in the San Juans

Western Safari Ranch
P.O. Box 128
Fairplay, CO 80440
800-530-8883 (reservations), 719-836-2431
Private 3,500-acre ranch; no trails; breakfast, lunch, and dinner rides; small guided groups and guided rides a specialty; open year-round

Windwalker Tours
P.O. Box 775092
Steamboat Springs, CO 80477
800-748-1642, 970-879-8065
Routt National Forest

The operations above offer trail rides of various lengths and often have pack trips as well. In addition, outfitters who specialize in setting up fishing and hunting camps can customize pack trips for backcountry photography, exploration, or simply enjoying the outdoors, especially in the nonhunting season when they may not be booked. An excursion with such an outfitter might be expensive, but it will also be comfortable, since most can supply relatively commodious wall tents with cots, a separate cooking and eating tent, and shower and sanitary facilities. Such outfitters can also do a "drop camp," where you provide everything you need, but the outfitter packs it in and out for you. A directory of outfitters and guides is available from:

Colorado Outfitters Association
P.O. Box 440021
Aurora, CO 80044
303-368-4731

INDEPENDENT PACKING

If you have an animal and are interested in horse or mule packing with it on your own, you can obtain equipment such as packsaddles, crossbucks, paniers, saddlebags, canteens, and other necessities from Brighton Feed, which also periodically offers classes in how to go about organizing and outfitting your excursion.

Brighton Feed & Farm Supply
370 North Main
Brighton, CO 80601
800-237-0721, 303-659-0721

CATTLE DRIVES

The horses are trained, wranglers serve as guides, and livestock is on the hoof—and anyone who's always wanted to play cowboy can live the fantasy. One-day cattle drives, perhaps starting with a chuck-wagon breakfast and usually including lunch on the range, are a uniquely Western adventure.

Black Canyon Ranch
76400 B-76 Road
Crawford, CO 81415
970-921-4252

Black Mountain Ranch
P.O. Box 219
4000 Conger Mesa Road
McCoy, CO 80463
800-967-2401, 970-653-4226

4 Eagle Ranch
4098 State Highway 131
Wolcott, CO 81655
970-926-3372

Overlook Ranch
P.O. Box 252
Craig, CO 81626
970-879-2606

Rocky Mountain Cattle Moo-vers
P.O. Box 457
Carbondale, CO 81623
970-936-9666

DUDE RANCHES

If you want to ride, ride, and ride some more, nothing beats a dude-ranch vacation. Colorado has forty of them, from the rustically elegant C Lazy 7, which has garnered Mobil Five Star and AAA Five Diamond honors, to the Focus Ranch, a working spread with 1,000 yearlings that guests help move from pasture to pasture. There's something to suit everyone's riding style, including instruction for children and adults. Although it has gained other meanings in

recent years, "dude" is an old term for a ranch guest from another region who pays for lodging, food, and use of a horse, though these days, ranches provide many more amenities. Hot tubs, swimming pools, tennis courts, fishing, four-wheel tours, and child care are available at many ranches. Many are open all winter and offer cross-country skiing and snowmobiling as well as riding. Ranch vacations can seem pricey, but generally they are all-inclusive, meaning that all meals and activities are included, and there are few additional charges. Guides to ranches and what they offer are available from:
Colorado Dude & Guest Ranch Association
P.O. Box 300
Tabernash, CO 80478
970-887-3128
Free guide to forty Colorado ranches

Dude Ranchers' Association
P.O. Box 471
Laporte, CO 80535
970-223-8440
$3.00 magazine guide to 101 ranches in the West, the majority in Colorado, Wyoming, and Montana

Old West Dude Ranch Vacations
c/o American Wilderness Experience
P.O. Box 1486
Boulder, CO 80306
800-444-DUDE, 303-444-2622
Tour operator specializing in Western ranch vacations

HORSEBACK RIDING FOR THE HANDICAPPED

Sheep Mountain Ranch Therapeutic Riding Center/
    YMCA of the Rockies
P.O. Box 1648
Granby, CO 80446
970-887-9271

LLAMA TREKS & HIKES

Llamas are the oldest known domestic animals, used by natives of what are now Peru and Ecuador for some 5,000 years. These congenial, surefooted animals with a soft, kind-to-the-earth step are ideal for Colorado's high country. Llama trekking falls somewhere between hiking and horse-packing. When you hike, you need to shoulder your own pack. When you horsepack, horses carry you and all the gear for your group. On a llama trek, you get to walk, but the beast has the burden. The rule of thumb is that llamas easily carry one-quarter to one-third of their body weight, which translates to seventy to eighty pounds, which again translates to more than the average backpacker is willing or able to carry at Colorado's altitude.

Like horse outfitters, some llama outfitters will lease their stock for a multi-day hike or arrange a drop camp for clients. Before going independently, it's important to be comfortable and knowledgeable in the backcountry, so that handling the llamas is the only new skill. Most outfitters and llama ranches that lease give half-day clinics on packing, loading, and staking llamas before a trip.

27

Information on llama trekking and other services is available from:
Colorado Llama Outfitters and Guides Association
30361 Rainbow Hills Road
Golden, CO 80401
303-526-0092

OUTFITTERS, AREAS, AND SPECIALTIES

Antero Llamas
11100 County Road 194
Salida, CO 8102
719-539-6405
Llama packing instruction; rentals

Ashcroft Llamas
Castle Creek Road
Aspen, CO 81612
970-925-1971
Lunch treks to Cooper Meadows at Ashcroft, American Lake, Cathedral Lake, or Tabor Lake

Backcountry Llamas
P.O. Box 1287
Paonia, CO 81428
970-527-3884

Buckhorn Llama Company
P.O. Box 64
Masonville, CO 8054
970-667-7411

Weminuche Wilderness; Rawah Wilderness; also early- and late-season trips to Utah's canyon country; day and lunch trips; lease programs; drop camps

Elk River Valley Llama Company
P.O. Box 674
Clark, CO 80428
970-879-7531
Operators of the llama program based at Keystone Resort

Home Ranch Llama Trekking
P.O. Box 8821
Clark, CO 80428
970-879-1780
Flat Tops Wilderness; special trips for fly-fishermen, women, singles, flora and fauna viewers, and fall foliage season

La Garita Llamas
32995 County Road 41G
De Norte, CO 82231
719-754-3345
La Garita Wilderness, Sangre de Cristo, and Weminuche trips; one-day and multi-day trips for families, women, recovery groups, and Quests (particular emphasis on spirituality in the wilderness)

Linda's Llama Land
167 Timber Ridge
Divide, CO 80814
719-378-2150 (summer),
719-852-5737 (winter)

Paragon Guides
P.O. Box 130
Vail, CO 81658
970-926-5299
Tenth Mountain Trail huts; White River National Forest

Pyramid Llama Ranch
P.O. Box 839
1258 County Road 19
Hayden, CO 81639
970-276-3348

Redwood Llamas
P.O. Box 518
Mancos, CO 81328
970-533-7835
Four- and five-day canyon-country treks; lunch hikes; lease
programs; drop hikes

Spruce Ridge Llama Treks
4141 County Road 210
Salida, CO 81201
719-539-4182
Full-day hikes and one- and two-night treks; specializes in
family outings

Steamboat Llama Ranch
4915 County Road 770/129
Steamboat Springs, CO 80487
970-879-8132

Timberline Llamas
30361 Rainbow Hills Road

Golden, CO 80401
800-859-8444, 303-526-0092
Colorado Trail; four wilderness areas; Front Range day and
picnic trips; also Wyoming's Wind River Range

Trail Skills
Lost Trail Ranch
Highway Contract No. 70, Box 7
Creede, CO 81139
970-852-5194

Wet Mountain Llamas
608 County Road 295
Wetmore, CO 81253
719-784-3220

For more information on the care, feeding, raising, and
use of llamas, contact:
Rocky Mountain Llama Association
P.O. Box 2347
Durango, CO 81302
970-247-1518

TIPS FOR RIDERS AND ANIMAL TREKKERS

What to Take

Long pants and a long-sleeved shirt if you are riding
through the woods will add immeasurably to the comfort
of a ride. Otherwise, all the skin protection and preparedness for Colorado's fickle weather are appropriate for riding or trekking with an animal. If you are organizing your

own pack trip, remember than most public lands now require that you use certified weed-free hay.

HOW YOU CAN HELP

The Network for Equestrian Trails of the Colorado Horsemen's Council calls on volunteers for its trail improvement projects:
Colorado Horsemen's Council
P.O. Box 1125
Arvada, CO 80001
303-279-4546, 303-499-3045 (Trails Network)

READING LIST

Gene Kilgore's Ranch Vacations by Gene Kilgore (Kilgore's Ranch Vacations, P.O. Box 1919,Tahoe City, CA 96145)
Horseman's Trail Book by Jan Schafer and Helen Egan (Red Ryder Enterprises, 430 North Independence Street, Lakewood, CO 80226)
North American Horse Travel Guide by Bruce McAllister (Roundup Press, P.O. Box 109, Boulder, CO 80306)
Packing With Llamas by Stanlynn Daugherty (Juniper Ridge Press, P.O. Box 1278, Olympia, WA 98507)

3 PEDAL POWER

Riders pedal ten-speeds, mountain bikes, touring bikes, and cross-breed bikes along thousands of miles of city streets, mountain roads, pass roads, bike paths, lumpy old mining and logging roads, disused railroad beds, auto roads on fourteeners, and single-track trails down ski mountains throughout Colorado. The census of designated trails and suitable routes is increasing so quickly that keeping track is impossible. You can take a bike trip independently or with an outfitter or fit some cycling in with other activities.

It seems that every Colorado resident has a bike or two, and many visitors bring their own. However, if you are of average size, you'll have no trouble finding a rental bike that fits, and many towns now seem to have more bike shops than T-shirt emporiums. Outfitters can provide bicycles for guided rides (sometimes they are included in the price), and shops all over the state rent quality equipment, including tandems, recombinant, and other specialty bikes. Children's seats and trailers make cycling a family sport, even if not all members are old enough to ride by themselves. Special events from fund-raisers to just plain fun dot the summer calendar, and Colorado regularly hosts big-time cycling competitions.

Bicycle Colorado, the leading general source for recreational cyclists, publishes a free annual magazine filled with useful information for cyclists. Join the organization and you get a free T-shirt, discounts on goods and services, updates on trail construction, and more.

Bicycle Colorado
5249 East Eastman Avenue
Denver, CO 80222
303-756-2535

Bicycling in Colorado, a free handbook to Colorado cycling laws, safety tips, and resources, is available from:
Colorado Bicycle Program
4201 East Arkansas Avenue, Room 225
Denver, CO 80222
303-757-9982

TYPES OF BIKES

The two most popular types in Colorado are lightweight, smooth-tired touring and road bikes for efficiency on paved roads, and sturdy, nubby-tired mountain bikes with low gearing designed for off-road cycling. Hybrids combining characteristics of each are up-and-comers because they are ideal for city riding and commuting.

CYCLING ON FEDERAL LANDS

Bicycling is permitted on roads and many trails in national forests and BLM land, but only on roads in national parks. The Forest Service and the BLM are engaged in an ongoing program to identify loops and routes suitable for mountain biking. Regional and local offices of both agencies have current information and maps.

WHERE TO BIKE

Boulder County

The city of Boulder is one of America's acknowledged cycling capitals and the hub of riding opportunities of all sorts. It seems as if every famous American road racer, with the exception of Greg LeMond and Lance Armstrong, lives or lived in this university town where bike shorts and jerseys are practically the local uniform. Boulder and its environs attract top cyclists because the long rides on the edge of the prairie and steep climbs up mountain roads provide exceptional conditioning.

In addition to the city's bike paths (described in the "Urban Rides" section), popular touring routes lead north of Boulder toward Lyons and Longmont, east to Lafayette and Erie, south on the fabled Morgul-Bismarck loop, and west into the mountains. Westward rides up (and back down) Flagstaff Road, Boulder Canyon, Fourmile Canyon, and Lee Hill Road are world-class routes for racers and exceptional conditioning rides for any strong and fit cyclist. Boulder also offers off-road trails, including a mellow old

narrow-gauge rail route called the Switzerland Trail; the
single-track Sourdough Trail; Caribou Flats; and Walker
Ranch, which all offer some climbs. Foothills Trail, Boulder
Valley Ranch Trail, and East Boulder Trail are easy and
nearly flat.

Boulder Convention & Visitors Bureau
2440 Pearl Street
Boulder, CO 80306
303-442-2911

Boulder County Bikeways
P.O. Box 471
2045 13th Street
Boulder, CO 80306
303-441-3900

Boulder Off-Road Alliance
1420 Alpine
Boulder, CO 80304
303-447-9378

Durango

This congenial town in southwest Colorado has few peers
and no betters when it comes to cycling. It provides access
to some of the best sections of the 425-mile Colorado Trail;
is the linchpin of the 236-mile San Juan Skyway loop,
which is a classic road cyclists' goal; is the nearest town to
the Purgatory Resort, with over thirty-six miles of top
mountain-biking trails; and is the gateway to limitless rides
through three million acres of San Juan National Forest

and BLM land. Annual events include the Iron Horse Bicycle Classic, the Bicycle Tour of the San Juans, the Durango Century Classic, and World Mountain Bike Week. (See also "Mesa Verde Country.")

Durango Chamber Resort Association
P.O. Box 2587
Durango, CO 81302
800-525-8855, 970-247-0312,
800-GO-DURANGO

Buffalo Creek Mountain Bike Area

Pike National Forest maintains an exceptional network of forty single-track and dirt-road bike trails for all ability levels, including a portion of the Colorado Trail. Many routes are smooth and rock-free, including a 15.8-mile loop to Buffalo Creek itself. The eight-mile Chair Rock ride is relatively easy and includes great views of dramatic rock formations, aspen groves, and mountain panoramas.

Pikes Peak Area Trails Coalition
P.O. Box 24
Colorado Springs, CO 80901
719-596-5640

Cañon City Area

With more than 330 days of sunshine annually, Cañon City styles itself as Colorado's climate capital. From flat trails, such as the Arkansas Riverwalk Tunnel Drive Trail (one mile), to demanding mountain-bike loops such as the sixty-five-mile, 4,400-foot-elevation-change circuit from Shelf Road to Victor, Phantom, Canyon, and back, this is an up-and-coming cycling area. Red Canyon Park offers thirty miles of moderate mountain-bike trails, with optional stops at the Garden Park Fossil Area and the Garden Park School, built in 1900. Many of the surrounding USFS trails are shared by bikers, hikers, and four-wheelers.

Cañon City Chamber of Commerce
P.O. Bin 749
Cañon City, CO 81215
800-876-7922, 719-275-2331

Craig Area

The remote and unspoiled northwestern corner of Colorado is the ancestral home of the Fremont people, the Utes, and a succession of outlaws, rustlers, and ranchers. Now it's being discovered by mountain and all-terrain cyclists who explore miles of unpaved roads throughout spacious and sparsely populated Moffat County. Popular rides include Elkhead Reservoir Recreation Area, the Black Mountain section of Routt National Forest, and Cedar Mountain Recreation Area, which all have miles of bike roads. In addition, the Yampa Valley Trail between Craig and Dinosaur is now being developed.

Greater Craig Chamber of Commerce
360 East Victory Way
Craig, CO 81625
800-864-4405, 970-824-5689

Crested Butte

This congenial resort in the heart of the Colorado Rockies is one of the state's true mountain-biking meccas (the town even houses the Mountain Bike Hall of Fame), and Fat Tire Bike Week each July is one of the holiest of seasons for fat-tire fiends. The country's oldest such festival started in 1976, before most people even knew there was such a thing as mountain biking, and it has grown ever since. The ski area runs two lifts to its trails, but the old roads that traverse the region provide an abundance of options. There's everything from the easy six-mile-around Mt. Crested Butte, with just 200 feet of elevation gain, to the twenty-two-mile, 3,200-vertical-foot lung-buster to Gunsight Pass.

Crested Butte–Mt. Crested Butte Chamber of Commerce
P.O. Box 1288
Crested Butte, CO 81224
800-545-4505, 970-349-6438

Fourteeners Region

Salida, Buena Vista, and Poncha Springs, a trio of towns strung along the temperate Arkansas River Valley, offer a long cycling season, hundreds of miles of mountain-biking routes, and outstanding scenery, particularly in autumn when the aspens turn gold and snow has started frosting the highest summits. Novices enjoy the relatively easy yet spectacular ride from Trout Creek Pass to Salida, via Bassam Park and Aspen Ridge, or the gentle Marshall Pass Road, an old railroad grade. Chalk Creek Canyon enables stronger riders to reach 13,000 feet on Hancock Pass, with stops in the historic mining town of St. Elmo and at chalk cliffs, waterfalls, and the Mt. Princeton Hot Springs. The Great Divide is a still more challenging combination of single-track, four-wheel-drive roads and gravel roads from the Monarch Pass summit to Poncha Springs, while the Monarch Crest Trail is twelve single-track miles along the Continental Divide at 10,000 to 12,000 feet. Banana Belt Fat Tracks, a local mountain-biking club, promotes riding in the region. The Monarch Mountain Challenge, a nationally sanctioned stage race, is reputed to be the nation's highest-altitude mountain-bike competition.

Chaffee County Visitors Bureau
P.O. Box 726
Salida, CO 81201
800-831-8594, 719-539-2459

Banana Belt Fat Tracks Mountain Biking Club
c/o Otero Cyclery
108 F Street
Salida, CO 81201
719-539-6704

Glenwood Springs

The completion of a smooth, eighteen-mile path that closely parallels the Colorado River eastward to Dotsero has cata-pulted Glenwood Springs into the forefront of neat places to bike. Spring Valley, Cattle Creek, and Missouri Heights are somewhat more challenging. Of the nearby mountain-biking trails that are considerably more rugged and far steeper, the top ones are Red Mountain, Transfer Trail, Bear Creek/Scout Trail, and Babbish Creek, the latter utilizing the cross-country ski trails at Ski Sunlight. All but the canyon ride can be combined or routed into loops.

Glenwood Springs Chamber Resort Association
1102 Grand Avenue
Glenwood Springs, CO 81601
970-945-1531

Grand Junction

The lush Grand Valley and the surrounding high desert of the Colorado Plateau provide a great variety of road- and mountain-biking options, and both have a kinder altitude and a warmer climate than the high mountains to the south and east. This translates into congenial mountain biking, especially early in spring and late in fall when the high country is nippy (and perhaps snowy). Cyclists share with vehicles the paved Colorado Riverfront Trail (see "Urban Rides" section) and the famous twenty-three-mile Rimrock Trail around Colorado National Monument. The scenic Rockcliffs north of the city and Grand Mesa National Forest, including the dramatic twelve-mile Lands End Trail to the east, both provide ample all-terrain and mountain-biking trails, including those at and near the Powderhorn ski area. The Grand Valley's vineyards and orchards offer wonderful opportunities to combine touring with tasting. Cycling the Colorado wine country is an annual late-May two-day tour.

Still, if this area were known for nothing else in mountain-biking circles, it would still be notable as the eastern end of Kokopelli's Trail, a landmark bike trail across the Colorado Plateau. Currently 128 miles long, it runs between Loma near Grand Junction and the mountain-biking mecca of Moab, Utah. A 325-mile loop is nearly completed. Already a legendary trail in this growing sport, Kokopelli is, in its entirety, a challenging endeavor. Still, some parts, including sections closest to Grand Junction, are relatively easy, with low elevations and no rigorous climbs.

Grand Junction Visitors & Convention Bureau
Horizon Drive
Grand Junction, CO 81506
800-962-2547, 970-244-1480

Colorado Plateau Mountain Biking Trail Association
  (COPMOBA)
P.O. Box 4603
Grand Junction, CO 81502
970-241-9561

Mesa Verde Country

The arid, rolling canyonlands and compelling Anasazi sites of southwestern Colorado near the Four Corners invite two-wheeled exploration. While summers can be brutally hot, there are fewer killer climbs than in the mountains. Combining cycling here with routes around nearby Durango (see above) provides a variety of terrain in one close area. Mesa Verde Country has some grandiose road routes of its own, notably the Cortez-Mancos-Dolores Half Century and the forty-eight miles of paved roads in Mesa Verde National Park. (Be sure to leave time to explore the storied Anasazi ruins.) Other, less famous ruins are best reached on a mountain bike, including Cannonball Mesa, Cutthroat Castle, Sand Canyon Pueblo, and the Mancos River Canyon, this last under the jurisdiction of the Ute Mountain Ute Tribal Park, which controls access and charges a fee (which, in turn, eliminates the crowds). Other fat-tire options include the thirteen-mile Railroad Loop, which combines an old railroad grade and a modern highway.

Mesa Verde Country Visitor Information Bureau
P.O. Box HH
Cortez, CO 81321
800-253-1616

Montrose

Road bikers cruise the thirty-five scenic miles of rolling land between this Uncompahgre Valley town and the Black Canyon of the Gunnison while mountain bikers explore miles of single-track and two-track routes through highland canyons. The 144-mile Tabeguache Trail between Montrose and Grand Junction is a top cycling route, as is the new ninety-five-mile Paradox Trail, which connects the Tabeguache and Kokopelli trails and creates the final link in the 325-mile loop route through western Colorado and eastern Utah.

Montrose Chamber of Commerce
550 North Townsend
Montrose, CO 81401
800-873-0244, 970-249-4534

San Juan Hut Trail

This 205-mile trail stretches from Telluride to Moab and links the alpine topography of Colorado's San Juan Mountains to the stark canyon and slickrock country of southern Utah. This high and scenic trail challenges strong mountain bikers who want to embark on a multi-day safari on two wheels. The main route is relatively wide, but single-track options abound for the fittest and most competent riders. Self-guided bikers can do the whole route in seven days on the trail and six nights in huts along the way that are provisioned with wood stoves, sleeping pads, blankets, and food. Each of the huts and walled platform tents is also accessible from intermediary trailheads, so that bikers without the time or the stamina for a week's ride at high altitude can select a shorter portion. The hut operator, who takes reservations for overnights, can also organize guided trips for those who prefer not to tackle it themselves. The San Juan Trail is generally bikable from May through September.

San Juan Hut Systems
P.O. Box 1663
117 North Willow Street
Telluride, CO 81435
970-728-6935

San Luis Valley

This broad valley between the San Juan and Sangre de Cristo mountain ranges is one of Colorado's unheralded cycling havens. It offers everything from a pancake-flat valley floor for ripping road biking to gonzo mountain passes topping 10,000 feet. Four hundred miles of roads twist through BLM lands, and an additional 2,800 miles of roads and 1,200 miles of trails in Rio Grande National Forest multiply cyclists' options. Additionally, there are two certified forty-kilometer time-trial courses for the serious racer.

San Luis Information Center
947 First Avenue
Monte Vista, CO 81144
800-835-7254

Steamboat Springs

The broad, scenic Yampa Valley makes for congenial cycling and includes the recently completed five-mile Yampa River Trail between Steamboat Springs and the Steamboat ski area. A short ride with a worthy goal is to proceed seven miles north of (and uphill from) town to the Strawberry Hot Springs, a series of rocky, spring-fed hot pools. After lazing in the hot water, about all you'll be good for is coasting back—and that's just what the return ride is. The ski area operates the Silver Bullet gondola for mountain bikers, who also can ride on miles of trails to the boundary of the Mt. Zirkel Wilderness in Routt National Forest and to nearby Rabbit Ears Pass, Steamboat Lake State Park and Recreation Area, and Pearl Lake State Park.

Steamboat Springs Chamber Resort Association
P.O. Box 774408
Steamboat Springs, CO 80477
800-922-2722, 970-679-0880

Summit County

Easily accessible from Denver on I-70, Summit County has fifty miles of paved paths suitable for road or mountain bikes. A ride around Lake Dillon is moderately demanding, but compensates with varied and sensational scenery. The smoothly paved six-mile bicycle path between Brecken-ridge and Farmers Corner near Frisco is an excellent family route, while the Copper Mountain–Vail Pass route, with its 1,500-foot elevation gain tempered by many switchbacks, is a good introduction to climbing and cruising for cyclists seeking more challenge.

In addition to these paved sections, ski lifts at Brecken-ridge, Keystone, and Copper Mountain ferry mountain bikes and riders uphill. The region's premier events for gonzo riders are Montezuma's Revenge, an annual twenty-four-hour mountain-bike odyssey crossing the Continental Divide nine times, and Pass Out, a one-day megaride of 205 miles with 16,250 feet of elevation gain. The annual Copper Mountain Criteriums are two days of high-powered racing on an eight-tenths-mile course each July, while September's annual Fall Classic offers two days of fat-tire thrills on the curvaceous trails of the Breckenridge Nordic Center.

Summit County Chamber of Commerce
P.O. Box 214
Frisco, CO 80443
970-668-5800

Telluride Area

The old mining roads surrounding Telluride are exceptional mountain-biking territory. Often challenging and always

46

scenic, they provide an up-close-and-personal relationship with the majestic San Juan Range. Ilium Road is a gravel byway leading to the Ames Power Plant, notable for being the first alternating current source in the country. Alta Lakes Road, Black Bear Pass, Last Dollar Road, and Tomboy Road to Imogene Pass are gonzo mountain routes, which cyclists must share with four-wheelers. Telluride also offers road warriors access to the ultra-beautiful San Juan Skyway, a significant ride feasible only on road bike powered by an extremely well-conditioned cyclist (see "Durango"). Easy in-town bike trips include the River Corridor Trail from Town Park to Boomerang Road and River Road along the San Miguel River.

Telluride Chamber Resort Association
P.O. Box 653
Telluride, CO 81435
970-728-3041

Tenth Mountain Division Trail

First built as a backcountry ski route across the spine of the Colorado Rockies, this noteworthy trail and its fabled huts are now also used for mountain biking. Some 300 miles of single-track trails and roads comprise the trail system, which surrounds the Holy Cross Wilderness. The average distance from trailheads to each of the dozen huts is eight miles, with elevation gains of up to 2,000 feet. Naturally, this requires good conditioning. Mountain bikers may reserve overnight hut space, camp out, or use the trail for day rides. The huts are also excellent jumping-off points for hikes into the adjacent wilderness, which is off-limits to bikes.

Colorado Outdoor Activity Guide

Tenth Mountain Division Hut Association
1280 Ute Avenue
Aspen, CO 81611
970-925-5775

Upper Rio Grande Valley

Bachelor Loop north of Creede is enough of a ride for some cyclists. It's twelve miles long and begins with about four uphill miles. But for others, it's just the start of a choice of such routes as San Luis Pass, Rat Creek, Upper West Willow, Equity Mine, and East Willow, the latter the region's most popular route. West Willow Route, with its demanding switchbacks, is mainly for well-conditioned riders. The annual Aspenfest includes a race on a fifteen-mile course combining Bachelor Loop and East Willow, which is also popular with recreational riders.

Creede–Mineral County Chamber of Commerce
P.O. Box 580
Creede, CO 81130
800-327-2102, 719-658-2374

Vail and Beaver Creek

These sister resorts are a commendable duo for cycling, with their in-town bike paths along Vail's Gore Creek, lift-served mountain biking on both Vail Mountain and Beaver Creek, guided tours, and miles of bike trails in the surrounding White River National Forest. Vail has hosted the

48

World Mountain Bike Championships, and you can ride three championship courses—Lionshead Loop, Village Loop, and Golden Peak Loop—individually or in combination. On Vail Mountain, the VistaBahn express chairlift and the Lionshead gondola run in summer, giving access to miles of fire roads, work roads, and single tracks. A special practice area for cyclists wanting to learn or practice mountain-biking skills is located near the top of the gondola, and eight-passenger sports-utility vehicles equipped for bikes shuttle bikers across the ridge atop the ski area, stopping at several drop-off points. Connie Carpenter-Phinney and Davis Phinney, two of America's most accomplished bicycle racers, have run their cycling camps in recent summers at nearby Beaver Creek; for camp information, call 800-859-8242.

Vail Resort Association
100 East Meadow Drive
Vail, CO 81657
800-824-5737, 970-476-1000

Vail Associates
P.O. Box 7
Vail, CO 81657
970-476-9090 (Vail), 970-949-9090 (Beaver Creek)

Winter Park/Fraser Valley

Winter Park is a great ski area in winter and a great mountain-biking area in summer. This resort, sixty-seven miles from Denver, is the heart of a 600-mile system of marked trails in Arapaho National Forest, the largest network of its kind in the country, with forty-four miles of lift-accessed trails at the ski areas connected with more than 550 miles on adjacent public land. Routes range from smooth roads to single-track plunges with the angles and wild turns of a roller coaster. Cyclists can muscle up mountains under their own power or take a chairlift up and cruise down. Winter Park's annual King of the Rockies Off-Road Stage Race and Mountain Bike Festival in late August is one of the sport's premier events for serious competitors and recreational cyclists.

Winter Park/Fraser Valley Chamber of Commerce
P.O. Box 3236
Winter Park, CO 80443
970-726-4118

GUIDED RIDES AND BICYCLE TOURS

Outfitters offer a variety of tours, including guided long-distance road trips complete with support staff and sag wagon; guided day and overnight mountain-bike tours; and drop trips, where the outfitter takes clients to a mountain-biking trailhead, summit, or pass and lets them make their way back at their own pace. All can supply bikes and helmets, and many also can provide rain ponchos and water bottles. Lunch is included in all full-day and many half-day trips, and longer trips include all meals. Most tours are scheduled regularly, while a few are available only once or twice a season.

OUTFITTERS, RIDES, AND SPECIALTIES

Aspen Bike Tours
P.O. Box 17781
Aspen, CO 81611
970-920-4059
Hunter Creek intro to off-road mountain-biking; Castle
Creek Road; downhill Lincoln Creek Road/Grizzly Reservoir

Back Country Biking
P.O. Box 2489
150 West Colorado Avenue
Telluride, CO 81435
800-828-7547 (Telluride Sports),
970-728-4477
Last Dollar Pass; single-track rides on Wilson Mesa, Deep
Creek, and Mill Creek Trails

Backcountry Biking
P.O. Box 886
Winter Park, CO 80482
970-726-4812
Blue Sky Tour for novice mountain bikers; other itineraries
for experienced riders

Challenge Unlimited
204 South 24th Street
Colorado Springs, CO 80904
800-798-5954, 719-633-6399
Multi-day itineraries such as Colorado Springs to Santa Fe,
Telluride to Moab, Colorado Springs–Cripple Creek–Cañon
City, and Tour des Aspens (foliage); mountain, all-terrain,
and road bikes

Colorado Recreational Adventures
7470 East Harvard Avenue, #L-207
Denver, CO 80231
303-368-8471
Low-cost, B.Y.O.B. (bring your own bike) tours in various
areas of Colorado

Cycle America
P.O. Box 29
Northfield, MN 55057
800-245-3263
Long-distance tours, including state-by-state, park-to-park,
regional, and coast-to-coast itineraries throughout the U.S.

Free Wheelin' Bike & Board
101 East Colorado Avenue
Telluride, CO 81435
970-728-4734
Mountain bike tours to Alta Lakes, Last Dollar Pass, and
Ilium Valley

Mad Adventures
P.O. Box 650
Winter Park, CO 80482
800-451-4844, 970-726-5290
Intro tours; van-up, bike-down tours

Mountain Bike Specialists
949 Main Avenue
Durango, CO
970-247-4066
Half-day to multi-day tours, from short, easy rides to longer

tours among the Anasazi ruins, Iron Horse route, and San
Juan Skyway

Mountain Man Tours
P.O. Box 11, Eagles Nest
Creede, CO 81130
719-658-2663 (May to October),
719-658-2843 (year-round)
Rio Grande National Forest; guided and drop trips

Mountain Tour Cycles
3365 North Academy Boulevard
Colorado Springs, CO 80917
719-596-8804
Pikes Peak region; mountain-bike tours

Paragon Guides
P.O. Box 130
Vail, CO 81658
970-926-5299
Tenth Mountain Division Trail hut tour

Roads Less Traveled
P.O. Box 8187
Longmont, CO 80501
303-678-8750
Rocky Mountain National Park; hut trips; specializes in
hike-and-bike combinations

Sawatch Naturalists & Guides
P.O. Box 53
Leadville, CO 80461

719-486-1856
San Isabel National Forest; road, mountain bike, and hut trips

Scenic Byways
P.O. Box 2972
Grand Junction, CO 81502
970-242-4645
Grand Valley tours, including Rimrock Drive and Lands End Trail, with overnights in a local hotel; winery and other specialty tours

Shrine Mountain Adventure
P.O. Box 4
Red Cliff, CO 81649
970-827-5363
Shrine Pass mountain bike tours

Sore Saddle Cyclery
1136 Yampa Street
Steamboat Springs, CO 80477
970-879-1675
Routt National Forest

SouthWest Adventures
P.O. Box 3242
780 Main Avenue
Durango, CO 81302
800-642-5389, 970-259-5370
San Juan Mountains

Sundance Mountain Adventures
P.O. Box 49304

Colorado Springs, CO 80302
800-972-2690, 719-593-5912
Challenging mountain-bike tours for the aggressive rider;
multi-day camping and hut tours, including Tenth Mountain Division Trail and Kokopelli's Trail

Tiger Run Tours
P.O. Box 1418
Breckenridge, CO 80424
970-453-2231, 303-623-3032 (metro Denver)
Arapaho National Forest

Timberline Bicycle Tours
P.O. Box 4382
Aspen, CO 81612
800-842-BIKE, 970-920-3214, 970-925-5773
Multi-day bike tours in and around White River National
Forest; multi-day mountain-bike trips for all ability levels

Two Wheel Tours
P.O. Box 2655
Littleton, CO 80161
303-798-4601
Multi-day tours including High Country Excursion from
Denver and San Juan Skyway from Telluride

Uncompahgre Bike Tours
P.O. Box 253
Ridgway, CO 81432
970-728-6935
Multi-day guided tours between Telluride and Moab utiliz-
ing San Juan Hut Systems huts plus wall tents

URBAN RIDES

Nearly one-third of the proceeds from the Colorado Lottery is mandated for recreational facilities, via the Colorado Division of Parks and Outdoor Recreation and the Conservation Trust Fund, which in turn distribute funds to cities and towns across the state. One of the favorite projects is for bicycle and multi-use paths, which are now paralleling rivers, winding through commercial and residential neighborhoods, and generally enhancing the quality of life of city dwellers and visitors.

Boulder

Bike-friendly Boulder is an environmentally conscious, congenial community with nearly forty miles of paved off-street paths that cyclists share with walkers, runners, and in-line skaters, plus 22.5 miles of well-marked bike lanes on city streets. More are under development. Boulder Creek Path, a seven-mile section passing through parks and wetlands, links the mouth of Boulder Canyon and its bike path with the eastern end of town. Boulder has embraced Colorado Bike Week, a July event to encourage cycling as alternative transportation.

Boulder Convention and Visitors Bureau
2440 Pearl Street
Boulder, CO 80301
303-442-2911

Colorado Springs

Sprawling Colorado Springs' web of designated bike routes encompass the city and its outskirts, including Manitou Springs, but the best cycling is in open-space areas. A bike route traverses the Garden of the Gods, a wonderland of red rock that's nature's finest sculpture gallery and one of the country's most fascinating city parks. Rampart Reservoir near Woodland Park has a mild twelve-mile route around the entire artificial lake, with dramatic rock formations along the shoreline and Pikes Peak looming above. The Santa Fe Trail is a scenic north-south bike route linking the U.S. Air Force Academy and the northern reaches of Colorado Springs with Palmer Park. The Santa Fe stretch features mountain views without mountain climbs, while Palmer Park has both primary and secondary trails.

Colorado Springs Convention and Visitors Bureau
104 South Cascade, Suite 104
Colorado Springs, CO 80903
719-635-7506

Denver

The city of Denver boasts 130 miles of trails, including loops in City and Washington Parks and connections to suburban ones, as well as marked bike lanes on streets throughout the city. Denver, which counts "Queen City of the Plains" among its nicknames, is largely an easy-riding flatland, but often flatland with wonderful mountain views. Many of the most popular trails, such as Bear Creek,

Cherry Creek, the Platte River Greenway, and the Highline Canal Trails, follow natural or man-made waterways. Others provide access to lakes and reservoirs, such as Berkeley Lake, Sloan Lake, and Cherry Creek Reservoir. In addition, biking through Denver enables cyclists to explore greenbelts, city parks, neighborhoods, and recreational areas.

For novice mountain bikers, it's hard to beat the 6.2-mile route through Waterton Canyon along the South Platte River southwest of Denver. Accessible from Chatfield Reservoir, just southwest of Denver, this section is also the easternmost leg of the Colorado Trail.

City of Denver Parks and Recreation Trails Program
945 South Huron Street
Denver, CO 80223
303-696-3901

Fort Collins

This northern Colorado college town has more than sixty miles of bike routes and, at this writing, a fourteen-mile multi-use asphalt path for cycling, jogging, and in-line skating, with more planned. The scenic stretches along the Cache La Poudre River are especially inviting, getting more use than any other park area in the city. The Spring Creek and Poudre River Trails can be combined into a relaxing twelve-mile circuit for mountain biking, while nearby Horsetooth Mountain Park and Lory State Park are connected by trail but not by road. Among their more challenging unpaved roads and single-track trails, the former's Horsetooth Rock Trail is a standout. Surrounded by country roads, Fort Collins is also an ideal center for chewing up the miles on a road bike, and biking of all sorts is so popular that one local store even rents only tandems.

Fort Collins Area Chamber of Commerce
225 South Meldrum Street
Fort Collins, CO 80522
970-482-3746

Pueblo

Located between challenging mountains and the calming grasslands, this southern Colorado city is developing a reputation as a fine place to cycle, with the thirty-five-mile Arkansas River Trail System providing an excellent two-wheel intro to the area. A 20.5-mile system of multi-use trails called the Pueblo Greenway River Trails is easy, while the connecting Fountain Creek and Lake Pueblo State Park are more challenging. Mountain bikers gravitate to the bluffs above Pueblo Reservoir for wonderful views without big hill climbs or descents. Touring bikes are the mode of choice for exploring the surrounding countryside. The Pedal Pueblo Century is a big annual road event, with options from twenty-five to 100 miles. A bonus is the moderate climate that makes comfortable cycling a real possibility, even in winter.

Pueblo Convention and Visitors Council
302 North Santa Fe
Pueblo, CO 81003
800-233-3446

DOWNHILL RIDES

For great views, fast-changing scenery, camaraderie, and minimal effort, Colorado's downhill bicycle tours can't be beat. Cycles and cyclists are transported to a mountaintop or other high spot and mostly coast downhill. Though most roads are paved, the upper portion of the Pikes Peak Highway is not. A mountain bike with good brakes, a helmet, rain and wind gear, a guide, a chase van to pick up stragglers, and at least a snack and sometimes lunch are included in the price.

OUTFITTERS, RIDES

Back Country Biking
P.O. Box 2489
150 West Colorado Avenue
Telluride, CO 81435
800-828-7547, 970-728-4477
Galloping Goose downhill tour on old rail bed, from Lizard Head Pass

Backcountry Tours
P.O. Box 886
Winter Park, CO 80482
970-726-4812
Blue Sky Tour (beginners back-road descent); Elk Meadow descent for riders with some experience

Blazing Pedals
P.O. Box 5929

Snowmass, CO 8161
800-282-7238, 970-923-4544 (Snowmass), 970-925-5651
　(Aspen)
Maroon Creek Road, Castle Creek Road

Challenge Unlimited
204 South 24th Street
Colorado Springs, CO 80904
800-798-5954, 719-633-6399
Pikes Peak (14,110 feet)

Mad Adventures
P.O. Box 650
Winter Park, CO 80482
800-451-4844, 970-726-5290
Blue Sky Tour (beginners back-road descent); Elk Meadow
descent for riders with some experience

Mountain Man Tours
Box 11, Eagles Nest
Creede, CO 81130
719-658-2663 (May to October),
719-658-2843 (year-round)
Rio Grande National Forest mountain roads, including
mine road through old mining districts

Telluride Outside
P.O. Box 685
666 West Colorado Avenue
Telluride, CO 81435
800-831-6230, 970-728-3895
Lizard Head Pass down Galloping Goose railroad route to
Ilium Valley

Timberline Mountain Bike Adventures
P.O. Box 4382
Aspen, CO 81612
800-842-BIKE
Half- and full-day tours of the Aspen area; hut tours using the Tenth Mountain Division Trail and Hut System

Trails and Rails
P.O. Box 217
1106 Rose Street
Georgetown, CO 80444
800-691-4-FUN, 970-569-2403,
303-670-1686 (metro Denver)
Clear Lake, Guanella Pass, Argentine Central, Mt. McClellan; Georgetown Loop Railroad ride option

Two Wheel Tours
P.O. Box 2655
Littleton, CO 80161
800-343-8940, 303-798-4601
Mt. Evans (14,260 feet); Vail Pass

MOUNTAIN BIKING AT SKI AREAS

When a ski area equips lifts to haul bicycles uphill in summer, mountain biking can be as tame or as tough as the rider chooses. Taking a lift to a high spot on the mountain makes many miles of unpaved roads and single tracks available to you so you can spend your time exploring a mountain rather than just climbing it on two wheels. The cost is modest, and rental bikes and helmets are available, too.

For inexperienced riders, there is always a very easy way down—and sometimes a guided group to join. Experienced riders love the vertiginous single tracks, and those who want to build stamina like to ride uphill as well as down. Beaver Creek, Copper Mountain, Crested Butte, Keystone, Powderhorn, Purgatory, Steamboat, Vail, and Winter Park (see the "Over the Snow" chapter for addresses and phone numbers) each operate one or two lifts for mountain bikers and hikers. Copper Mountain traditionally does not charge to ride its lifts in summer.

LONG TRAILS

In addition to Kokopelli (see the "Grand Junction" listing in "Top Cycling Areas"), the Tenth Mountain Division and San Juan Trail and Hut Systems (see the "Over the Snow" chapter for details) are for mountain bikers as well as hikers and skiers. The Colorado Trail (see the "Afoot" chapter) is also accessible to mountain bikes.

ANNUAL TOURS AND EVENTS

Not for the casual rider, Colorado offers an unsurpassed selection of annual races, rallies, hill climbs, mountain-bike festivals, centuries (100-mile rides), and multi-day marathons for the exceptionally well-conditioned cyclist. Some are fund-raisers for medical or environmental charities, providing challenges for a good cause. The list below is but a small sampling of the races and rallies around the state.

May

East Valley Orchard Ramble
Palisade Chamber of Commerce
P.O. Box 729
Palisade, CO 81525
970-464-7458
Twenty- and 25-mile routes through blooming orchards and rolling countryside of western Colorado

Tour of the Arkansas River Valley
Colorado Springs Cycling Club
P.O. Box 49602
Colorado Springs, CO 80949
719-594-6354
Two-day, 185-mile tour from Cañon City to Buena Vista; highlights are the Arkansas River Valley and Pike National Forest

Iron Horse Classic
P.O. Box 1389
Durango, CO 81302
970-259-4621
Memorial Day weekend race, established in 1971, as road race pitting riders against the Durango & Silverton Narrow Gauge Railroad; now huge event with mountain bike and cross-country divisions, plus various specialty classifications

June

Courage Classic
c/o The Children's Hospital
1056 East 19th Avenue

Denver, CO 80218
303-447-2106
Three-day, 144-mile road tour for intermediate and expert riders though Rocky Mountain National Park; Trail Ridge Road is the highest continuous paved road in the world (the Mt. Evans road is higher but dead-ends near the summit); limited to 2,000 riders; includes free luggage transfers, free showers, free camping, and special rates at hotels and motels

Ride the Rockies
1560 Broadway
Denver, CO 80202
303-820-1338
Six-day trans-mountain tour limited to 2,000 riders (chosen by lottery); route varies but includes high passes, long stretches, and overnights in various ghost towns; length is roughly 500 miles with an elevation gain of some 20,000 feet

Fat Tire Classic
Winter Park Resort
P.O. Box 36
Winter Park, CO 80482
970-726-5514
Two-day mountain bike tour around Winter Park; each day is about 20 miles

July

Fat Tire Bike Week
P.O. Box 782

Crested Butte, CO 81224
800-545-4505, 970-349-6817
Mountain-bike festival in late July; instructional clinics; choice of daily tours; bicycle rodeo; bicycle polo; two-day stage race; Interbike Cycling Film Festival

Steamboat Bike Challenge
Steamboat Springs Chamber Resort
P.O. Box 774408
Steamboat Springs, CO 80477
800-922-2772, 970-879-0880
Two-day event with hilly and technical mountain terrain; road and all-terrain bicycle events up to 100 miles; limited to 500 riders

August

Arvada Century
c/o North Jeffco Foundation
9101 Ralston Road
Arvada, CO 80002
303-424-7733
Street course of 100 hilly but not mountainous miles; 25- and 50-mile options, plus six-mile family loop; limited to 900 participants

King of the Rockies
c/o Winter Park Resort
P.O. Box 3236
Winter Park, CO 80482
800-453-2525, 303-447-0566 (metro Denver)

Serious mountain-biking competition for pros and amateurs
highlights five-day festival; clinics, guided mountain rides,
observed trials, food, and festivities

September

Bicycle Tour of the San Juans
c/o Iron Horse Classic
P.O. Box 1389
Durango, CO 81302
970-259-4621
Three-day tour with road (206- and 239-mile options) and
mountain (74 miles with 12,200 feet of elevation gain); fully
supported; limited field (maximum of 75 mountain bikers)

Tour de Hardscrabble Century
Colorado Springs Cycling Club
P.O. Box 49502
Colorado Springs, CO 80949
719-594-6354
100 miles; San Isabel National Forest and Sangre de Cristo
road tour via Hardscrabble Pass

Bike to Nature
c/o Volunteers for Outdoor Colorado
1410 Grant Street, Suite B-105
Denver, CO 80203
303-830-7792
Two-day rally in Pike National Forest with back-road and
single-track options; includes party and entertainment

TIPS FOR CYCLISTS

Many of the preparedness tips for hikers and backpackers (see the "Afoot" and "Out for the Night" chapters) are applicable to cyclists as well, specifically: have sunglasses or other protective eyewear; take enough water; take rain- and windproof clothing; and take sunscreen and lip balm. Gloves, either bike gloves or flexible windproof designs such as cross-country skiing gloves, can make the difference between pleasure and pain on a cycling trip. Colorado has no helmet law, though outfitters require them and all prudent cyclists wear them.

When sharing roads with cars, might makes right, and safe cycling demands obeying traffic laws and more. Stay in the bike lane or on the right shoulder, signal for turns, and never hitch onto a moving vehicle. When riding in the backcountry, stay on designated trails and be religious about respecting private property, trail closures, wetlands, tundra, and other fragile off-road areas. It is best not to ride when trails are wet or muddy, but if you must, ride through the mud, not around it, which widens the trails. Leave gates surrounding grazing land as you found them. Yield to uphill riders, and when encountering hikers or especially horses, dismount or slow down to let them pass.

What to Bring

Self-sufficiency is necessary in the backcountry and advisable on road tours (except for guided rides where the support van takes care of contingencies). Be sure to take energy snack bars, sunglasses, suitable maps, and compass.

Many riders like a rear-view mirror on helmet or handle-bars. For your bike, you'll want at least a pump, tire levers, tube-patch kit, spare tube, and tire boot. Also recommended are chain lubricant, chain tools, small screwdriver, and a set of fixed, adjustable, and Allen wrenches.

READING LIST

The Best of Colorado Biking Trails (Outdoor Books, P.O. Box 417, Denver, CO 80201)

Bicycle Touring Colorado by Dennis Coello (Northland Publishing, P.O. Box N, Flagstaff, AZ 86002)

Bike With a View by Mark Dowling (Concepts in Writing, 1135 South Garfield, Denver, CO 80210)

Colorado Cycling Guide by Jean and Hartley Alley (Pruett Publishing, 2928 Pearl Street, Boulder, CO 80302)

Colorado Gonzo Rides by Michael Merrifield (Blue Clover Press, Monument, CO 80132)

Mountain Biking Colorado's Historic Mining Districts by Laura Rosseter (Fulcrum Publishing, 350 Indiana Street, Golden, CO 80401)

4 PADDLE POWER

For the adventurous, Colorado's fast-flowing rivers and tranquil lakes are best experienced from a kayak or a canoe. Mobility, freedom, and, in the case of whitewater paddling, the rare sense of constantly testing self against the elements are the appeals of these activities. River kayaking is a high-intensity sport that brings a real adrenaline rush. Kayakers talk about "playing" the water, not just navigating thrilling rapids but also stalling the kayak in water conditions such as stoppers and standing waves.

Instruction is important for any level of river kayaking and crucial to surviving whitewater. It should cover learning how to do basic and later advanced strokes, reading rivers, knowing what constitutes safe versus dangerous passages, and performing special skills. Most introductory courses are divided into pre-river and on-river segments. The pre-river curriculum may include dry land and/or lake instruction. The Eskimo roll, an advanced skill necessary for whitewater, is often taught initially in a pool. Racing is kayaking's ultimate extension.

If river kayaking is for thrill seekers, lake canoeing is the opposite—a calm, Zen-like activity, as well as an efficient mode of water transportation that enhances fly-fishing and camping. Canoeing doesn't take extraordinary skill, just a little practice to do it efficiently. In addition to the specialty shops and outfitters below, a number of raft companies also offer whitewater instruction and equipment for beginners. Since much of the information on rivers, seasons, equipment and clothing needs, and other details of interest to rafters is also applicable to kayaking, see the "Afloat" chapter for the basics.

The Colorado Whitewater Association attracts kayakers, rafters, and canoeists with a wide range of programs and activities. CWA organizes kayak instruction for beginners and intermediates, organizes whitewater cruises on rivers throughout Colorado every weekend from May to August, issues a newsletter, sponsors river-safety programs and kayak races, and lobbies for the preservation of free-flowing rivers and against unfair river closures. Members of the Rocky Mountain Canoe Club are enthusiasts of all sorts of paddling sports, but mostly canoeing. The club holds meetings, schedules several trips a year, issues a newsletter, and offers introductory training by certified American Canoe Association instructors.

Colorado Whitewater Association
P.O. Box 4315
Englewood, CO 80155
303-430-4853

Rocky Mountain Canoe Club
P.O. Box 280284
Lakewood, CO 80228
303-693-2109

TYPES OF BOATS

Native peoples have used kayaks and canoes on North American waters for millennia, but only recently, with high-tech materials and Americans' growing quest for adventure, have they become popular for sport and recreation. With miles of rivers and scores of reservoirs and lakes, landlocked Colorado is surprisingly well appointed for water sports.

The traditional Eskimo kayak has been reincarnated as a maneuverable, lightweight craft for a paddler sitting in an enclosed cockpit; tandem models are also available. Because of its extreme sensitivity, this type of boat requires balance and skill, but these characteristics also make it tops for serious paddlers in search of serious whitewater. The paddler who tips over such a kayak will be upside down in the water and needs to do the Eskimo roll to get upright again. This is probably kayaking's best-known maneuver, the one that gives it a reputation as a gonzo sport. Kayaks in different lengths and widths for paddlers of different sizes, with ends that may be pointed, stubby, or in between for various kinds of water, with keels and without, are specifically configured for whitewater, lake, or sea use. Some models feature hatches for food, fishing equipment, or other gear and perhaps even an ice-chest holder, making them ideal for day trips. Kayakers use double-bladed paddles.

Sit-on-tops are user-friendly boats most suitable for lakes, but whitewater models with drain holes are also available. The paddler who falls into the water just needs to jump back on and start stroking again. Inflatable kayaks, nicknamed "duckies," also come in solo or tandem models. They are the simplest to use and suited for powerful whitewater. In fact, experts say it takes less skill to move a duckie through the rapids than a kayak. One outfitter even offers unique Russian-made paddle-cats, side-by-side craft for two paddlers.

Canoes, derivative of birch-bark models paddled by Indians and those old camp models paddled by many American youngsters, consist of a rigid open-topped hull in which one or two paddlers sit. Designed for stillwater reservoirs and lakes, recreational canoes are stable and sturdy. Cruising canoes are the freighters of paddling sports, suitable for hauling cargo to a campsite by the side of a lake or stream. Whitewater canoes are impact- and abrasion-resistant, designed to be maneuverable for running rapids. Versatile canoes are the closest design to an all-purpose boat, capable of hauling some cargo and yet adequate for some whitewater. Canoe paddles are single-bladed.

WHERE TO KAYAK

Colorado's major rafting rivers are all exemplary kayaking venues as well, but because kayaks are smaller than rafts, they can be maneuvered in rocky narrows, smaller streams, and upriver sections where rafts cannot go. Even private individuals are required to have permits on most rivers, and they are available from the Bureau of Land

Management or the U.S. Forest Service. Colorado's streams are public property, open to anyone who wants to float through. This is not so with the riverbanks and even some riverbeds, however, and kayakers must respect private-property signs. As is the case with raft trips, horseback trips, backcountry ski tours, and many of Colorado's other outdoor activities, a kayak trip with an outfitter provides a permit, plus convenience, equipment, and the virtual assurance of the success and safety of the adventure that guided activities always offer.

Much to the distress of those who oppose taming the natural course of a river, many of Colorado's rivers are dammed. Sometimes the dams inhibit running whitewater, and sometimes they enhance it, but they're a fact of life, so river-flow reports are also a fact of life. For recorded information on cubic feet of flow per second on all the rivers within the Colorado River Basin, Green River Basin, Great Basin, and San Juan Basin, call 801-539-1311. The Colorado Division of Water Resources has assembled detailed flow information on some 200 stretches of rivers in Colorado. For a list of the codes needed to access "Water Talk," write to 1313 Sherman Street, Room 818, Denver, CO 80203. Then call 303-831-7135 for updated "Water Talk" reports. TravelBank Systems of Colorado also includes stream flow in its lexicon of information, accessible via computer and modem at 303-671-7669.

Slalom courses are set up seasonally on rivers in a handful of Colorado cities and towns, including the Arkansas River in Salida, Boulder Creek in Boulder, the Yampa River in Steamboat Springs, the North Platte in Denver, and the Animas in Durango. These courses do not require a permit. FIBArk (which stands for First in Boating on the Arkansas) is an event that generally takes place during four days in mid-June when snowmelt swells the Arkansas. It is reputedly the world's most challenging whitewater event for kayakers and canoeists. For information, call 719-539-6193 or 719-539-4847.

WHERE TO CANOE

In addition to the rivers that appeal to whitewater canoeists as much as to kayakers, many of the state's lakes and reservoirs are open for public recreation. When regulations for a specific reservoir or lake indicate that "boating" is permitted, that's a green light for canoeing. Nevertheless, canoeists who prefer not to be buzzed should choose sites that permit "boating" but not "motorboating" or "personal watercraft" (i.e., Jet Skis). Also note that some sites are closed during late fall, the migratory-waterfowl season, generally from November 1 through the heart of winter, when canoeing is not pleasant anyway.

Reservoirs that prohibit motorized boats include Aurora Reservoir southeast of Denver, Barbour Ponds east of Longmont, Barr Lake southeast of Brighton, John Martin Reservoir east of Las Animas, La Jara Reservoir southwest of Monte Vista, North Sterling Reservoir north of Sterling, Spinney Mountain Reservoir east of Hartsel, and Williams Fork Reservoir east of Parshall. Motorboats are prohibited in mountain lakes, too, but only those with practical vehicle access make canoeing easy. These include Brainard, Lefthand Creek Reservoir (gasoline-powered boats prohibited), Long Lake, Moraine Lake, Rainbow Lakes, and Red Rock Lake, all in Roosevelt National Forest in western Boulder County. Summit Lake in the Arapaho National Forest and Abyss Lake in the Pike National Forest, both near Georgetown, are also near roads. Nonmotorized boats are also permitted in more than thirty small mountain lakes under Roosevelt National Forest jurisdiction in two dozen lakes in the Arapaho National Forest, and in six lakes in the Pike National Forest. Since these are all back-country lakes, they are accessible only to those with a strong back and the determination needed to carry canoes or inflatables.

OUTFITTERS, PROGRAMS, AND OTHER DETAILS

American Adventure Expeditions
P.O. Box 12844
US 285 and 24
Buena Vista, CO
800-288-0675, 719-395-2409
Kayak instruction for all levels; river trips

Aspen Kayak School
P.O. Box 1520
Aspen, CO 81612
907-925-4433
Weekend to week-long courses and trips

Boulder Outdoor Center
2510 North 47th Street
Boulder, CO 80301
800-364-9376; 303-444-8420
Whitewater instruction; lake and river trips and canoe and kayak instruction; canoe and kayak rentals

Centennial Canoe Outfitters
P.O. Box 440307
Aurora, CO 80044
303-755-3501
Largest canoe outfitter west of the Mississippi; guided river trips; clinics on reservoirs and lakes; Front Range theme trips for singles, women, families, bird-watchers, and other special groups

Colorado Canoe Trippers
c/o Blazing Paddles
P.O. Box 5929
Snowmass, CO 81615
800-282-7238, 970-923-4544 (Snowmass), 970-925-5651
    (Aspen)
Guided intro-to-canoeing trips

Crested Butte Kayaking and Adventures
P.O. Box 2779
Crested Butte, CO 81224
970-349-1323

Dvorak's Kayak & Rafting Expeditions
17921-B U.S. 285
Nathrop, CO 81236
800-814-3795, 719-539-6851
Whitewater school (including teen whitewater skills camp); multi-day trips

Moondance River Expeditions
310 West First Street
Salida, CO 81201
719-539-2113

River trips featuring Russian paddle-cats, unique paddle-catamarans for two or four paddlers; first (and perhaps still only) U.S. outfitter carrying these boats; instruction

Mountain Sports Kayak School
P.O. Box 771198
Steamboat Springs, CO 80477
970-879-8794, 970-879-6910 (evenings)
Instruction, specializing in beginners; Yampa and Colorado River day and multi-day trips

Osprey Adventures
P.O. Box 1937
810 Main Street
Frisco, CO 80443
970-668-5573
Canoe tours, instruction, and rentals

Outdoor Connections
38 Tucker Street
Craig, CO 81625
970-824-5510
"Unguided" river trip with shuttle; rentals

The Paddle Shop
1727 15th Street
Boulder, CO 80302
303-786-9940
Kayak instruction at all levels on lakes and rivers

Raven Adventure Trips
P.O. Box 108
Granby, CO 80446

800-332-3381, 970-887-2141
Kayak instruction and river trips

Rocky Mountain Adventures
P.O. Box 1989
Fort Collins, CO 80522
800-858-6808
970-493-4005 (Fort Collins), 970-586-6191 (Estes Park),
    719-395-8594 (Buena Vista)
Whitewater instruction

Rocky Mountain Diving Center
1737 15th Street
Boulder, CO 80302
303-449-8606
Ocean kayak rentals and basic instruction

Barry Smith's Mountain Sports Kayak School
P.O. Box 1986
Steamboat Springs, CO 80488
970-879-8794 (days), 970-879-6910 (evenings)
Specializes in beginning kayaking instruction

Steamboat Kayak School
c/o Backdoor Sports
P.O. Box 774703
841 Yampa Avenue
Steamboat Springs, CO 80477
970-879-6249
Beginning and advanced instruction; rentals

Three Rivers Resort
P.O. Box 339

130 County Road 742
Almont, CO 81210
970-641-1303
Kayaking instruction; guided trips using inflatables

Wazzoo Canoe Outfitters
P.O. Box 109
Golden, CO 80402
303-237-6632
Instruction; day and multi-day trips; environmental and executive river trips

TIPS FOR KAYAKERS AND CANOEISTS

For whitewater paddlers, all the tips and cautions given for rafters apply—multiplied, because there is no boatman to compensate for the individual paddlers' lack of skill or absence of caution and good sense.

What to Bring (and What Not To)

Again, the same basic lists apply to paddlers as to rafters, but with a few additions and modifications. Because kayakers are closer to the water, they need to be even more conscious about protective clothing. Very early in the melt-off season, some kayakers wear maximum-warmth drysuits. Later, bib-model wetsuits become popular. These do not have arms, and since Neoprene tops designed for scuba diving would be too restrictive for intense paddling, waterproof jackets designed for paddling are available. When temperatures are chilling, gloves are a plus.

A life preserver, also called a PFD (for *personal flotation device*), is a must. It would be folly to be on the river without one, and many agencies administering reservoirs and lakes require them, too. By tradition, kayakers all wear protective helmets, but canoeists do not.

READING LIST

Class Fire Chronicles by Jeff Bennett (Swiftwater Publishing, P.O. Box 3031, Portland, OR 97208)

Colorado: Rivers of the Rockies by John Fielder and Mark Pearson (Westcliffe Publishers, Inc., 2650 South Zuni Street, Englewood, CO 80110)

San Juan Canyon: A River Runner's Guide by Don Baars and Gene Stevenson (Canon Publishers, 411 Lawrence Avenue, Lawrence, KS 66044) and *Dolores River Guide* by Ralph DeVries and Stephen G. Maurr (Southwest Natural and Cultural Heritage Association, Drawer E, Albuquerque, NM 87103) cover one river each. Many of the books in the "Afloat" chapter are also suitable for kayakers and canoeists.

Westwater Books (P.O. Box 2560, Evergreen, CO 80439) publishes extensively mapped, individual guides to the Green River, Dinosaur National Monument, and the Desolation Wilderness by Lois Belknap Evans and Buzz Belknap.

The Whitewater by Richard Penny (Mesaha Ridge Press, P.O. Box 59257, Birmingham, AL 35259)

Whitewater Kayaking by Ray Roe (Stackpole Books, P.O. Box 1831, Harrisburg, PA 17105)

5
AFLOAT

Running Colorado's big rivers is nothing new. Native peoples and early trappers and mappers long traveled inland waterways. In 1869, John Wesley Powell, the one-armed Civil War veteran, commanded four wooden boats to be put in on the Green River in what is now Wyoming. The Powell party set off on the Green, continued down the Colorado, and discovered the Grand Canyon three months later. The rapids were lethal to four of Powell's seven men and two of the boats, but the turbulent, churning sections of whitewater that were a menace in the last century are the highlight of many a river trip in this one.

Colorado's most scenic and exciting rivers provide everything from white-knuckle rides in early spring to gentle summer floats suitable for families and those timid about the water. Some rivers and streams run free, offering challenging whitewater adventure; others are dammed, providing a more consistent flow throughout rafting season and more scenery than thrills and chills.

Rafting gets into gear in May, just after skiing season ends, when run-off from prodigious snow accumulations pours down from the high mountains and fills rivers and streams. When the skiing season is good, the whitewater will run high and the rafting will be great, too. Whitewater season peaks in mid-June, but rafting opportunities stretch through October, though not all rivers or river sections can be run all season long. Outfitters offer trips that extend from half-day floats to multi-day expeditions, complete with camping, meals, and the opportunity to explore some of the surrounding country. Depending on the rivers and the lands they pass through, outfitters and their guides may have licenses or permits from the Colorado State Parks Department, the U.S. Forest Service, or the Bureau of Land Management.

Nearly half a million people each year put themselves in the hands of Colorado raft guides, called boatmen (no matter which gender). A boatman's qualifications to handle rafts and take passengers on specific classes of whitewater depends on experience, measured in numbers of hours on the river, and all boatmen are trained in whitewater seamanship, first aid, and rescue. Whether a trip is for a half-day, two weeks, or anything in between, the routine always starts with an equipment and safety briefing. Expect at least one drive, often by old school bus, from the meeting place to the put-in, from the take-out to the meeting place, or both. Full-day trips include lunch; multi-day trips include three meals a day.

Many commercial raft companies are members of a trade association that operates as a clearinghouse for information on whitewater adventures.

Colorado River Outfitters Association
P.O. Box 1662
Buena Vista, CO 81211
970-369-4632

TYPES OF RAFTS

Recreational rafting traces its origins back to 700-pound Army surplus rafts and assault boats. Now maneuverable, self-bailing rafts as light as 100 pounds make rafting an adventure for all ages. Two basic types of rafts are now in use: paddle boats and oar boats. On a paddle boat, the boatman is stationed at the back, reading the river, fine-tuning the steering with one long oar, and calling directions to the passengers, who also act as crew. A paddle boat, which typically carries eight to ten people, is active and fun. The boatman shouts commands ("Right side forward, left side back paddle," "Everyone forward," "Rest"), and clients provide the muscle.

On an oar boat, the boatman sits on a raised seat in the center, powering and steering the raft with two long oars. The passengers are just that, sitting and gazing at the passing scenery. Because oar boats can haul a lot of freight, they are popular for multi-day trips, but because clients tend to get bored, many outfitters also stock inflatable kayaks, nicknamed "duckies," for use on milder rivers. Each duckie holds one or two people, who are encouraged to float downstream close to the mother ship. Occasionally, outfitters mount a fleet of oar boats, duckies, and motor-assisted rafts. Some outfitters combine two popular sports with float trips down excellent fishing streams.

FAMILY RAFTING

Since commercial outfitters run only milder river stretches, a raft trip is a suitable family adventure, and because prices include meals and camping gear and there are few distractions on the river, an excellent value as well. Most outfitters offer reduced prices for children (usually to age twelve); some offer generous discounts (up to half-off) and occasionally, a children-raft-free offer materializes. Companies that specialize in family trips are particularly mindful of both children's fears and their desire for some adventure. Since youngsters often like to get splashed and scared a little, but not a lot, family-oriented outfitters know how to show youngsters the excitement of whitewater without terror.

Outfitters often have minimum-age guidelines for specific trips, but as a rule of thumb, figure that children as young as three are usually fine on a Class I or II trip, which is essentially a float, while seven-year-olds generally find a trip with moderate rapids just great. A family with smaller children might prefer an oar boat, where the boatman handles the chores, while older children might want to participate in the thrill of a paddle boat.

CLASSES OF RIVERS

A simple five-step scale, designated in Roman numerals, describes rivers under normal conditions and the skill needed to negotiate them. It is important to remember, however, that water fluctuations affect these ratings:

Class I—Easy—Small waves; no experience required

Class II—Medium—Moderately difficult rapids; clear passages

Class III—Difficult—Waves numerous, irregular, and high; rocks, eddies; requiring expert skills in maneuvering

Class IV—Very Difficult—Long rapids; waves powerful; irregular boiling eddies; powerful, precise maneuvering required

Class V—Extremely Difficult—Large and violent rapids; highly congested routes almost always requiring scrutiny from shore; critical and complex maneuvering required

WHERE TO RAFT

A brochure called "BLM Colorado River Adventures," with a good map, river classifications, average gradient, trip length, and other useful information on most of Colorado's top rafting rivers is available from the Bureau of Land Management (see Appendix for addresses). Outfitters have procured permits for specific stretches of rivers, but independent rafters need them, too. See the Paddle Power chapter for details.

Animas River

Trips of the spectacular and challenging upper Animas in southwest Colorado begin outside the old mining town of Silverton, with mostly Class IV and a few Class V rapids, while those on the lower Animas begin in Durango, to the south, and proceed through the Southern Ute Reservation.

The lower Animas is far gentler and is suitable for family floats of just an hour or two, a congenial option available on very few Western rivers. The Durango & Silverton Narrow Gauge Railroad parallels the river, and at least one train passes rafting parties each day, with rafters and rail-roaders greeting and photographing each other. The train is also used to shuttle rafters around a narrow, wild-water gorge between the upper and lower Animas that is considered unnavigable by any kind of craft.

Arkansas River

In its first 125 miles, the Arkansas River tumbles 5,000 vertical feet, a stretch that includes the single most popular rafting area in the United States. The Headwaters Recreation Area includes both the upper Arkansas, between Leadville and Cañon City, and the lower Arkansas, from Salida to Parkdale. Put-ins near Leadville, Buena Vista, Salida, Vallie Bridge, Parkdale, Cañon City, and Pueblo Reservoir provide access to sections of river that are truly for everyone, with trips that range from short, mild floats for the very young or very timid to long, lung-busting, muscle-straining whitewater excursions.

Brown's Canyon, eight miles south of Buena Vista, is considered by many the state's whitewater capital. With Class III rapids between granite boulders and views of the Collegiate Peaks, this twenty-five-mile stretch is a good half- or full-day trip, and numerous outfitters specialize in it. The Numbers, a stunning twenty-one-mile section punctuated with Class V rapids, is ultra-exciting. Parkdale, a twenty-three-mile stretch of Class III and IV rapids, has been nicknamed the Grand Canyon of the Arkansas, but many people consider the best part to be the twenty-two-mile run through Royal Gorge, which has the most impressive scenery and Class III and IV rapids.

Because of its popularity with rafters and kayakers, plus the pressure from anglers and from those interested in the Arkansas as a water source, a protective organization for this splendid river has been formed. In late 1990, the Bureau of Land Management announced a study of the upper Arkansas for possible designation as a National Wild and Scenic River, which would prohibit dam construction. The study motivated the city of Colorado Springs to file for rights to build two dams, which would flood over three miles of river, reduce downstream river flows by nearly a third, and scar the scenic landscape with dam construction and pipelines. For a state-of-the-Arkansas report, or to help protect the river, contact:

Friends of the Arkansas
P.O. Box 924
Buena Vista, CO 81211
719-395-6416

Blue River

Located in Summit County, less than two hours from Denver, the Blue offers a combination of scenery and Class III thrills. The raftable portions are at an altitude of about 9,000 feet, so as the Blue tumbles along a high valley, it offers both vistas of rugged mountains and whitewater stretches that are some of the closest to the Front Range. The Blue is usually run on half- and full-day trips.

Cache La Poudre

The Cache La Poudre in north central Colorado was the first river in the state designated as a National Wild and Scenic River, and at this writing, still the only one in Colorado with this protection. Flowing down the east side of the Continental Divide, it boasts Class III and IV rapids on the upper stretches and gentles out to easy sections downriver. Often referred to simply as the Poudre, the river is uncrowded, scenic, and convenient to Denver, Boulder, and Fort Collins.

Colorado River

With headwaters in Rocky Mountain National Park, the Colorado is a modest stream for many miles before becoming boatable around Kremmling. This section of the upper Colorado, with Class I to III rapids, is a good choice for families, seniors, beginners, and tentative rafters. It runs through the Gore Mountain Range, whose majestic canyons, lush meadows, and fertile ranchland valleys provide scenery and variety. One- to four-day trips are offered.

Downriver, east of Glenwood Springs, the Colorado cuts through the dramatic Glenwood Canyon. Concrete put-in ramps make this eighteen-mile stretch one of the easiest river sections to access in Colorado. It is scenic but not isolated because rafters share the canyon with Amtrak and freight trains, motorists and truckers on I-70, and cyclists and joggers on a new recreation path along the water.

The lower Colorado flows through brilliant deserts with

spectacular rock formations and memorable colors. Just as it reaches the Utah line, it slices through a series of stunning canyons with Class III and IV rapids. Ruby Canyon is unusual because it can be run year-round. Ruby and Horsethief Canyons are milder, while Westwater Canyon is both more dramatic and challenging. A stretch containing seven breathtaking canyons comprising the Black Ridge Canyons Wilderness Study Area have been recommended for designation as National Wild and Scenic Rivers.

Dolores River

The Dolores flows from the high country of the San Juan Range through the dramatic canyon lands of southwest Colorado. Multi-day trips are the rule of this river. Most are two to three days long, but they can be combined into a longer expedition. The most famous part of Ponderosa Canyon, with Class III and IV whitewater, is Snaggletooth Rapid. Sandy beaches and towering ponderosa pines characterize this forty-seven-mile section. Slickrock Canyon contains fifty-eight miles of Class II and III river through sandstone walls and towers. The forty-five miles of Hanging Flume Canyon couples Class III rapids with a gentle four-mile float through the Paradox Valley with its giant cottonwood trees and great blue heron rookeries. When the San Miguel joins the Dolores, water volume typically doubles, so the whitewater ratchets up to Class III and IV through Gateway Canyon and Beaver Canyon shortly before the confluence with the Colorado River.

Eagle River

The upper Eagle near Vail offers the excitement of Class IV to V rapids, while the lower Eagle is great for families and first-time rafters. The forty-mile stretch of the Eagle most popular for half- and full-day trips slices through wondrous, multi-hued sandstone canyons and is also known for good wildlife-spotting opportunities. Dowd Chute, where Gore Creek spills into the Eagle, is a splendid stretch of white-water thrills.

Green River

The Green River, in the spectacular high desert of north-west Colorado, makes for fascinating two- to four-day float trips with a handful of mild rapids. Because the raftable section of the Green is in a largely roadless area, the stark and beautiful landscape is best seen from the water. Flaming Gorge Reservoir controls the water flow, making for consistent rafting and a long season, and the Browns Park section just below the dam is a popular Class I and II section for fishing floats. The ninety-six-mile stretch through Desolation Gray Canyon is an easy Class I to III float through remote wilderness. Starting with the splendid Lodore Canyon, which offers relatively easy but exhilarating rapids, usually Class II and III, and ending in Dinosaur National Monument, the Green is an excellent choice for families and *Jurassic Park* fans. Optional side trips are walks to memorable ancient Anasazi petroglyphs at a couple of sites, and dinosaur-loving youngsters enjoy the opportunity to dig for fossils once they've dried off.

91

Gunnison River

Gorgeous Gunnison Gorge, northeast of Montrose, has been nicknamed "Baby Grand." This deep chasm of the upper Gunnison is accessible only to hikers, horseback riders, and river travelers, so it has a true backcountry atmosphere. Formally known as the Gunnison Gorge Wilderness Study Area, this segment has been recommended for designation as a National Wild and Scenic River.

Class III to IV rapids make the fourteen-mile gorge a thrilling ride. One-, two- and three-day trips are usual, not because this is a long stretch of river, but because there are so many possibilities for diversion. Rafters may spot bighorn sheep, elk, deer, and migratory waterfowl, and the trout fishing is Gold Medal. The lower Gunnison is considerably milder, yet while its Class I and II rapids make it ideal for the timid, it's not dull. Views from the river range from the scenic Dominguez Canyon to pastoral vistas of ranches and orchards.

North Platte

This scenic river begins in North Park, a wide valley near the Wyoming border. Northgate Canyon is the river's finest whitewater stretch, with Class III and IV rapids, and is suitable for one- to three-day trips. The region is known for ranching, a profusion of wildlife and wildflowers, and solitude.

Rio Grande

The 1,897-mile Rio Grande is the second-longest river in the continental United States, with headwaters in the mountainous heart of Mineral County. Still, it is not considered a major Colorado rafting river because the best stretch in the state is relatively short and comparably tame. Thirty miles of easy-floating water through beautiful countryside studded with sagebrush, pinion pine, and juniper make the Colorado portion of the Rio Grande a serene experience. It is therefore a good river for rafters who want to refine their skills by renting their own craft, rather than joining an outfitter. The toughest section is Box Canyon, below Rio Grande Reservoir, with Class IV and V water. For the most part, however, the river's thrills come from sightings of deer, elk, beaver, muskrat, eagles, and falcons.

Yampa River

This fantastic, untamed river in northwest Colorado has been called "the last of the wild ones." Class III and IV rapids abound, with the Warm Springs section often cresting to Class V in peak season. Since water levels depend entirely on run-off, the snowmelt pattern rather than a dam engineer determines the depth of the river and the force of the flow. As it's the last of the free-flowing rivers, trips tend to fill up fast with purists who want to run a river as they all once were.

OUTFITTERS

Most but not all companies belong to the Colorado River Outfitters Association (see above), which offers a free booklet on the member firms and their programs. Outfitters generally specialize in frequent (often daily) trips on nearby rivers and may also offer a handful of multi-day excursions to them and also to more distant rivers.

OUTFITTERS, RIVERS

A Wanderlust Adventure
P.O. Box 976
Laporte, CO 80535
800-745-7238, 970-484-1219
Cache La Poudre, Dolores

Acquired Tastes, Inc.
Mid-May to September:
27410 Colorado State Highway 319
Buena Vista, CO 81211
719-395-2992
September to mid-May:
2053 Yarmouth
Boulder, CO 80301
303-443-4120, 800-888-8582 (year-round)
Arkansas

A-1 Wildwater, Inc.
317 Stover Street
Fort Collins, CO 80524
800-369-4165, 970-224-3379
Cache La Poudre, Arkansas, North Platte, Dolores

Adventure Bound River Expeditions
2392 H Road
Grand Junction, CO 81505
800-423-4668, 970-5633
Green, Yampa, Colorado

Adventures Wild Rafting
P.O. Box 774832
Steamboat Springs, CO 80477
800-825-3989, 970-879-8747
Colorado, Eagle, Yampa, Arkansas, Cross Mountain

American Adventure Expeditions
P.O. Box 1549
12844 US 285 and 24
Buena Vista, CO 81211
800-288-0675, 719-395-2409
Arkansas, Animas

Arkansas River Tours/Four Corners Rafting
P.O. Box 1032-B
Buena Vista, CO 81211
800-332-7238, 719-395-4137 (May to early September)

Blazing Paddles
P.O. Box 5929
Snowmass, CO 81615
800-282-7238, 970-923-4544 (Snowmass),
970-925-5651 (Aspen)
Arkansas, Colorado, Roaring Fork

Boulder Outdoor Center
2510 North 47th Street
Boulder, CO 80301
800-364-9376, 303-444-8420
Cache La Poudre

Breckenridge Whitewater Rafting
P.O. Box 980
402 Main Street
Frisco, CO 80443
800-247-RAFT, 970-668-5323
Colorado, Arkansas, Eagle, Clear Creek

Buffalo Joe River Trips
P.O. Box 1526
113 North Railroad Street
Buena Vista, CO 81211
800-356-7984, 719-395-8757, 303-798-1386 (metro Denver)
Arkansas, Dolores

Buggywhip's Fish & Float Service
P.O. Box 770479
Steamboat Springs, CO 80477
800-759-0343, 970-879-8033
Yampa, Colorado, Green, North Platte, Eagle, Arkansas

Canyon Marine Whitewater Expeditions
P.O. Box 545
129 West Rainbow Boulevard (US 50)
Salida, CO 81201
800-643-0707, 719-539-7476
Arkansas

Clear Creek Rafting
Heritage Square, Building U, #2
18301 West Colfax Avenue
Golden, CO 80401
303-277-9900
Clear Creek, Colorado, Eagle, Arkansas

Colorado Riff Raft
P.O. Box 4949
55 East Durant
Aspen, CO 81612
800-759-3939, 970-925-5405 (Aspen), 970-923-2220
    (Snowmass)
Arkansas, Roaring Fork, Colorado

Colorado River Runs
Star Route, Box 32
Bond, CO 80423
800-826-1081, 970-653-4292
Colorado, Arkansas

Crested Butte Rafting
P.O. Box 1306
Crested Butte, CO 81224
800-445-6639, 970-349-7423
Gunnison, Taylor, Lake Fork, Arkansas, Colorado, Piedra

Durango Rivertrippers
720 Main Avenue
Durango, CO 81301
970-259-0289
Animas

Dvorak Kayak & Raft Expeditions
17921-B U.S. 285
Nathrop, CO 81236
800-824-3795, 719-539-6851
Arkansas, Colorado, Dolores, Green, Gunnison

Echo Canyon River Expeditions
45000 U.S. 50 West
Cañon City, CO 81212
800-748-2953, 719-748-2953
Arkansas, Gunnison, Lake Fork, Piedra, San Miguel

Don Ferguson's Whitewater Rafting
1280 Ithaca Drive
Boulder, CO 80303
800-597-4861, 303-494-0824
Arkansas

Flexible Flyers Rafting
2344 County Road 225
Durango, CO 81301
970-247-4628
Animas

Four Corners Rafting
P.O. Box 1032
Buena Vista, CO 81211
800-332-RAFT
Arkansas

Good Times Rafting & Joni Ellis River Tours
P.O. Box 1588
Buena Vista, CO 81211

800-477-0144, 970-453-5559 (Summit County),
970-468-1028
Arkansas, Blue

Sheri Griffith River Expeditions
P.O. Box 1324
Moab, UT 84532
800-332-2439, 801-259-9226
Colorado, Green

Gunnison River Expeditions
P.O. Box 315
Montrose, CO 81402
800-297-4441, 970-249-4441
Gunnison, Black Canyon/Gunnison Gorge, San Miguel

Don Hatch River Expeditions
P.O. Box 1150
Vernal, UT 84078
800-342-8243, 801-787-4316
Yampa, Green

Independent Whitewater
P.O. Box B
Monarch, CO 81227
800-428-1479, 719-395-2642
Arkansas (Brown's Canyon only)

Keystone Resort
P.O. Box 38
Keystone, CO 80435
800-451-5930, 970-468-4180
Arkansas, Colorado, Blue, Eagle

KODI Rafting & Bikes
P.O. Box 1215
Breckenridge, CO 80424
800-525-9624, 970-453-2194,
303-453-9241 (metro Denver), 719-395-2700 (Buena Vista)
Arkansas, Colorado, Blue

Lazy J Resort & Rafting Co.
P.O. Box 109
16373 U.S. 50
Coaldale, CO 81222
800-678-4274, 719-942-4274
Arkansas

MAD Adventures
P.O. Box 650
Winter Park, CO 80482
800-451-4844, 970-726-5290
Clear Creek, Colorado, Arkansas

Monarch Guides
P.O. Box 967
Kremmling, CO 80459
800-882-3445, 970-653-4210
Colorado, Eagle

Moondance River Expeditions
310 West First Street
Salida, CO 81201
719-539-2113
Arkansas; particularly environmentally conscious outfitter
with organically grown food served on river trips

Mountain Man Tours
Box 11, Eagles Nest
Creede, CO 81130
719-658-2663 (May to October),
719-658-2843 (year-round)
Rio Grande

Mountain Waters Rafting
P.O. Box 2681
108 West Sixth Street
Durango, CO 81302
800-748-2507, 970-259-4191
Animas, Piedra

Noah's Ark Whitewater Rafting Co.
P.O. Box 850
Buena Vista, CO 81211
719-395-2158
Arkansas

Pagosa Rafting Outfitters
P.O. Box 222
Pagosa Springs, CO 81147
970-731-4081
Piedra, Animas, San Juan

Peregrine River Outfitters
64 Ptarmigan Lane
Durango, CO 81301
970-385-7600
Piedra, Animas, San Juan, Colorado

Performance Tours Rafting
P.O. Box 7305
110 Ski Hill Road
Breckenridge, CO 80424
800-328-7238, 970-453-0661
Arkansas, Blue, Colorado

Raftmeister
P.O. Box 1805
Vail, CO 81657
800-274-0636, 970-476-7238.
Eagle, Arkansas, Colorado

Rapid Transit Rafting
P.O. Box 4095
Estes Park, CO 80517
800-367-8523, 970-586-8852, 970-586-2303
Colorado, Cache La Poudre

Raven Adventure Trips
P.O. Box 108
Granby, CO 80446
800-332-3381, 970-887-2141
Colorado, Arkansas, North Platte

River Runners, Ltd.
11150 U.S. 50
Salida, CO 81201
800-525-2081, 719-539-2144
Arkansas

Riverswest
520 Main Avenue
Durango, CO 80301
800-622-0852, 970-259-5077
Animas, Piedra

Rock Gardens Rafting
1308 County Road 129
Glenwood Springs, CO 81601
970-945-6737
Colorado, Roaring Fork

Rocky Mountain Adventures
P.O. Box 1989
Fort Collins, CO 80522
800-858-6808, 970-493-4005
Cache La Poudre, Arkansas, Colorado, Dolores, North Platte

Rocky Mountain Outdoor Center
10281 U.S.50
Howard, CO 81233
800-255-5784, 719-942-3214
Arkansas, Dolores

Rocky Mountain Tours
P.O. Box 3031
12847 South U.S. 285 and 24
Buena Vista, CO 81211
800-551-5140, 719-395-4101 (summer),
719-579-9145 (Colorado Springs, year-round)
Arkansas

Scenic River Tours
703 West Tomichi Avenue
Gunnison, CO 81230
970-641-3131, 970-641-4205 (evenings)
Gunnison, Arkansas, San Miguel, Colorado

SouthWest Adventures
P.O. Box 3242
780 Main Avenue
Durango, CO 81302
800-642-5389, 970-259-5370
Animas, Piedra

Tenth Mountain Sports
P.O. Box 251
322 Harrison Avenue
Leadville, CO 80461
800-892-6371, 719-486-2202
Arkansas

Three Rivers Resort
P.O. Box 339
130 Colorado State Highway 742
Almont, CO 81210
970-641-1303
Gunnison, Taylor, Lake Fork

Timberline Tours
P.O. Box 131
Vail, CO 81658
800-831-1414, 970-476-1414
Eagle, Arkansas, Colorado

Timberwolf
7330 West U.S. 50
Salida, CO 81201
800-843-8448, 719-539-7508
Arkansas, Dolores

Twin Lakes Expeditions
P.O. Box 70
Colorado State Highway 82
Twin Lakes, CO 81251
800-288-0497, 719-486-3928
Arkansas, Lake Creek

Whitewater Encounters, Inc.
1422 South Chambers Circle
Aurora, CO 80012
800-530-8362, 719-539-7478 (Buena Vista), 404-751-0161
Arkansas

Whitewater Odyssey
P.O. Box 2186
Evergreen, CO 80439
800-674-3637, 303-674-3637
Arkansas, Rio Grande, North Platte, Colorado

Whitewater Rafting
P.O. Box 2462
Glenwood Springs, CO 81602
970-945-8477
Colorado, Roaring Fork

Whitewater Voyageurs
P.O. Box 346
Poncha Springs, CO 81201
800-255-2585, 719-539-7618
Arkansas

Wilderness Aware, Inc.
P.O. Box 1550
Buena Vista, CO 81211
800-462-RAFT, 719-395-2112
Arkansas, Dolores, North Platte, Gunnison, Colorado,
Piedra, Animas

RAFTING FOR THE DISABLED

Most raft companies can customize or modify a trip for
special needs, and disabled rafters can also participate in
floats and trips with easy put-ins and take-outs. Arkansas
River Tours/Four Corners Rafting and Moondance River
Expeditions (see above) are especially accommodating.

TIPS FOR RIVER TRIPS

What to Bring

For your feet, take tennis shoes that you're willing to soak,
river sandals (socks underneath will protect your ankles
from sunburn, and if they're wool, they'll provide warmth
as well), or Neoprene booties. For the body, a wetsuit is
practically mandated when the air and water temperatures
added together total less than 100 and preferred by many

rafters at any time. Otherwise, nylon or other fast-drying synthetic shorts, a shirt, and a windbreaker are recommended for a river trip. Dry clothes to change into add to après-rafting comfort. Surprisingly, rain gear is a good idea, too. It's common to wear swimwear under clothes. Wear a hat with chin strap and sunglasses with retainer strap.

For the skin, carry insect repellent, sunscreen, and lip protector; for the family album, bring a camera, preferably a water-resistant or disposable waterproof one. For possessions you must bring along but want to protect, take a dry bag (found in sporting-goods stores) or sealable plastic bags. For overnight trips, bring along long pants and a long-sleeved wool sweater, a sweatshirt and/or jacket for cool evenings, dry shoes for camp, a flashlight, a towel, and personal toiletries. And don't forget some money to tip the boatman. Some outfitters include and/or rent wetsuits, booties, rain gear, tents, and sleeping bags.

What Not to Bring

Forget the leather shoes, blue jeans, or any cotton clothes that stay wetter and colder than synthetics, valuables such as credit cards or jewelry, or anything that absolutely must stay dry. While some outfitters permit beer or other alcoholic beverages (particularly to consume at dinnertime on overnight trips), some do not, so check with the company.

SAFETY TIPS

It is mandatory, gospel, required, commanded, THE LAW always to wear a personal flotation device (a.k.a. lifejacket) on the river. They are designed so that a person will float face up, and most even have extra flotation at the neck so that the head is raised. There will be an orientation before the trip, which everyone should pay attention to, and the boatman will be properly equipped for emergencies and will go through the necessary safety procedures, but it's always good for everyone to know the drill.

Here's what to do in the unlikely event of trouble on the river. If you fall out, don't panic. Listen to the boatman, who will call instructions to you. If your lifejacket doesn't automatically float you on your back, get into that position and maneuver your body so that your feet are downstream and your toes are up. Remember to breathe as much as possible. If you are in the rapids, breathe between waves but close your mouth in the peaks. Look around. If the raft is upstream, get away from its path so that you are not caught between it and an obstacle downriver from you. If the raft is downstream, allow yourself to drift down to it so that the boatman can maneuver around to help you. If a rope is thrown to you, hold it over your shoulder, lie on your back, and let the rescuer pull you in.

HOW YOU CAN HELP

With its miles of raftable rivers, Colorado is a leading participant in National River Clean-Up Week, usually the second or third week in May. Public and private agencies, commercial and private boaters, outdoor retailers, and other volunteers cleaned up more than 230 miles of river in 1994. For information, call America Outdoors National River Clean-Up at 615-524-4814 or a Colorado River Outfitters Association representative at 719-942-3214.

READING LIST

Colorado River Recreation by Dirksen McKinney (Recreational Sales Publishing, P.O. Box 1028, Aptos, CA 95501)

Colorado's BLM Wilderness: Hiking & Floating by Mark Pearson and John Fielder (Westcliffe Publishers, Inc., 2650 South Zuni Street, Englewood, CO 80110)

The Floaters Guide to Colorado by Doug Wheat (Falcon Books, P.O. Box 1718, Helena, MT 59624)

Rivers of Colorado by Jeff Rennicke (Falcon Books)

The Upper Arkansas River by Frank Staub (Fulcrum Publishing, 350 Indiana Street, Golden, CO 80401)

Western Whitewater by Jim Cassady, Bill Cross, and Fryar Calhoun (North Fork Press, P.O. Box 3580, Berkeley, CA 94703)

Whitewater Rafting in Western North America by Lloyd D. Armstead (Globe Pequot Press, 6 Business Park Road, Box 833, Old Saybrook, CT 06475)

6 AFOOT

There is no finer way to discover Colorado's magic than step by step. Colorado offers walking paths and hiking trails for all levels of conditioning and comfort, from easy ambles on broad paths beside urban rivers to grueling scrambles up steep slopes to sky-high summits. The high country invites exploration and impels people to put one foot in front of the other until they reach a goal—a panoramic viewpoint, a lake, a ghost town, a pass, or a mountaintop. En route, hikers may enjoy profuse wildflowers and, with luck, spot some wildlife as well.

Trailheads dot Colorado and trails crisscross the state. Some are right off major highways close to cities or resort towns; others branch off from harrowing four-wheel-drive roads and lead deep into the remote wilderness. Trails vary in length, from handicap-accessible paths of less than a mile to mega-marathons along the crest of the Rockies, and in challenge, from easy family strolls to arduous uphills that are just short of technical climbs, requiring ropes and other protective paraphernalia.

Still, anyone who is reasonably fit and acclimated can ascend even Colorado's highest peaks. There's oxygen-sapping elevation to contend with, and tricky summer weather as well, but virtually every mountain has at least one hike-up route. For the most part, technical rock climbing is strictly optional. You can hike independently or in organized, guided groups with a commercial outfitter or a membership organization of like-minded outdoor enthusiasts for security and companionship.

WHERE TO HIKE

FOURTEENERS

California's Mt. Whitney, at 14,494 feet above sea level, is the highest mountain in the continental United States, but that state's thirteen "fourteeners" are a fraction of Colorado's fifty-four. Because Pikes Peak is so famous, many people who think it is Colorado's highest mountain are surprised to learn that thirty others are higher. "Peak bagging," a term describing successful summit ascents, and "bagging" fourteeners are the ultimate goal of many Colorado hikers. In fact, some 50,000 people a year reach the state's highest summits, and fourteeners have achieved such mythic (and commercial) status that they've inspired specialized hiking and climbing guidebooks, T-shirts, and logs in which to note the date, conditions, and companions for every ascent.

All hikers remember their first fourteener, and while many are content to have completed just one, others aren't

111

happy until they've climbed all fifty-four, climbed them all in a year, climbed them on consecutive days, climbed them in winter, or all of the above. What the top of every four-teener offers, whether it's your first or your fifty-fourth, is a sense of being on top of the world and the pride of getting there one step at a time. (See Appendix for a complete list of the fourteeners and their elevations.)

WILDERNESS AREAS

The most pristine, roadless sections of Colorado's national forests and national parks are gradually being designated as wilderness areas. The designation means that human activity is strictly limited: no logging, no mining, no per-manent structures or commercial enterprises (such as backcountry huts or yurts, or ski areas, as are permitted beyond wilderness boundaries). Permitted recreation in-cludes hiking, backpacking, backcountry skiing, snowshoe-ing, and fishing, but mountain biking, hang gliding, and using motorized vehicles are prohibited.

AREAS FOR DAY HIKES

Crested Butte Area

Crested Butte is a charming Victorian town with a contem-porary ski resort nearby. For hikers, these serve as a con-venient base for the surrounding wilderness areas. You can pick your trail from the short but easy, like the 2.5-mile Ute Pass Trail, or the long but easy, like the 6.5-mile Oh-Be-Joyful Road leading to Blue Lake. If steep is your desire, try the Daisy Pass Trail or Trail #403 between Washington Gulch and East River. Crested Butte is at the southern end of the Maroon Bells–Snowmass Wilderness, and hikes in the direction of Aspen via a choice of high, scenic passes are among Colorado's top routes. Less widely known wilderness areas are the West Elk Wilderness and Raggeds Wilderness, just west of Crested Butte. The Crested Butte area also lies on the "backside" or west of the Collegiate Peaks Wilderness. The Crested Butte–Mt. Crested Butte Chamber of Commerce (800-545-4505, 970-349-6438) puts out a good overview map of area trails.

Flat Tops Wilderness

This huge wilderness area straddles Routt and White River National Forests and contains some of the best areas of both. Flat Top Mountain, peaking at 12,500 feet, is the namesake summit. The Beaver River Trail is an easy three-miler from the north shore of Stillwater Reservoir to the headwaters of the Bear River, with an option of continuing into the tundra to Trappers Lake. Lost Lakes Trail is nearly 5.5 miles of high-mountain hiking through great stands of spruce and fir.

Gore Range

The Gore Range's craggy ridges and spiky peaks are among the most admired mountains by even the most hurried travelers, since much of the range is located between I-70 and US 40. Some of the best sections are within Eagles Nest Wilderness. Numerous trailheads provide access

113

to this seventy-mile-long range, which is located in the Arapaho and White River National Forests.

The southern access to the rambling Gore Lake Trail is just six miles from Vail, and strong hikers can combine it with a side trip to Red Buffalo Pass. Several fine trails begin in the Piney River Valley, including the most hiked route to Mt. Powell, which, at 13,560 feet, is the highest summit in the range. Various sections of the 54.5-mile Gore Range Trail can be done as day hikes. The South Gore Range stretches south of I-70 toward Leadville. Numerous summits of 12,000 feet or more, the popular routes at Shrine Pass, Camp Hale trails, and the northernmost section of the Tenth Mountain Trail are in this range.

Indian Peaks Wilderness

The Indian Peaks stretch between Rocky Mountain National Park and Rollins Pass. Their crest is the Continental Divide. The wilderness area, created in 1978, is the most frequently visited in the Rocky Mountain region and one of the most popular in the country. Of the forty-nine noteworthy summits, 32 are over 11,000 feet in elevation. Ten of the most prominent peaks were named after Indian tribes. The wilderness is crossed by some 130 trails, which lead to the summits, countless high-mountain lakes, and year-round snowfields (including Arapahoe Glacier, North America's southernmost glacier), which make this a mountain area of spectacular beauty.

The most heavily used trails are those above the Brainard Lake Recreation Area (since 1994, Brainard has been a fee area), but the weekend pressure of Front Range hikers is great on all the eastern trails throughout the summer. For more solitude, start at one of the western trailheads. The southern portion features the remnants of an old railroad line, and the Needles Eye Tunnel, now caved in and closed, which once linked Rollinsville and Winter Park. High peaks such as Audubon, Arapahoe, and Mt. Toll lure strong hikers, but most visitors can easily walk to such easy-access, lower-elevation lakes such as Mitchell, Long, and Blue.

Maroon Bells–Snowmass Wilderness

To many people, the spectacular Maroon Bells–Snowmass protection area is Aspen's doorstep wilderness. So popular is the Maroon Lake access that the auto road is closed to most private vehicles during the summer, and visitors must ride in by bus. The lake is the site of one of the world's most photographed mountainscapes and also offers congenial family trails. The rest of the wilderness area, which comprises the heart of the Elk Range, is hidden from view except to hikers.

One of the easier hikes is on Maroon Creek Trail, a 3.25-mile downhill from Maroon Lake to East Maroon Portal. By contrast, East Maroon Creek Trail is 8.5 miles of uphill challenge through wildflower meadows and up steep slopes to East Maroon Pass at 11,820 feet, with the option of continuing down the other side and flying back from Crested Butte. (Arrange a van shuttle with Town Taxi, 970-349-5543, and a flight with Aspen Aviation, 970-925-3445.)

The Elk Range boasts six fourteeners, all of them demanding: Capitol, Castle, Pyramid, Maroon Peak, North Maroon Peak, and Snowmass. Many experts consider

Capitol to be the most challenging of all the fourteeners. Other, less demanding but extremely worthwhile hiking destinations include American Lake and Cathedral Lake.

Additional trails and mountains are found on the Crested Butte, or south, side of the Elk Mountains (see below). Remnants of mining activity add interest to many hikes. A number of peaks exceed 12,000 feet, and several top 13,000. To reach a high elevation without climbing the entire distance, take a Crested Butte chairlift and climb roughly a thousand feet to the namesake mountain's 12,162-foot summit. It is also possible to hike East or West Maroon Pass or Pearl Pass, which separate the Crested Butte Elks from the Aspen Elks.

Mt. Zirkel Wilderness

This exquisite wilderness northeast of Steamboat Springs is a magnificent area of peaks and high lakes, deep forests, tundra, and two significant rivers (the Elk and the Encampment, both of which have been proposed for National Wild and Scenic River designation). The whole is laced with hiking trails. Its attributes are so obvious that it became one of the five original areas designated by the Wilderness Act of 1964. You might think of it as one of the mothers of Colorado's wilderness bounty.

Several of the most popular day hikes have lovely mountain lakes as their destinations. The Gold Lake Trail is a moderate 2.8 miles, the Three Island Lake Trail is 3.4 miles, and, at nearly five miles, the Gilpin Lake Trail terminates at the Continental Divide. Perhaps the most stunning of these lake hikes, however, is the Rainbow Lake Trail, 3.5 moderate miles culminating at the largest lake

116

in the wilderness. The Mt. Zirkel hike itself is taxing, with nearly 4,000 feet of elevation gain, but for those with endurance and skill, the route past the old mining ghost town of Slavonia to the three-peaked mountaintop produces a satisfying day hike.

Rocky Mountain National Park

Rocky Mountain National Park probably would not exist if not for a nineteenth-century snow surveyor named Enos Mills and *Wild Life on the Rockies,* his book about the lofty countryside he knew so well and loved equally. This preserve of spectacular high-Alpine scenery, little more than an hour from Denver, contains 124 named peaks above 10,000 feet (including 102 over 11,000 feet, seventy-nine over 12,000, twenty over 13,000, and one, spectacular Longs Peak, over 14,000). Nowhere is the range and variety of Colorado's high country more visible. Though it has no single compelling feature like Yellowstone's Old Faithful or Yosemite's Halfdome, Rocky Mountain's deep glacier-carved valleys, sheer granite cliffs, perpetual snowfields, high mountain cirques, and vast stretches of Alpine tundra make this one of America's most magnificent parks.

Winters are so harsh that Trail Ridge Road, the continent's highest continuous paved road, which bisects the park, is generally snowed in well before Thanksgiving and isn't plowed out again until Memorial Day. The park's 355 miles of trails range from short paved stretches suitable for wheelchairs or strollers to steep multi-milers. Longs Peak, whose distinctive flat summit crests at 14,255 feet, is most hikers' first truly challenging fourteener. Most people must start before sunrise, and many don't finish the nearly fifteen-mile, 5,000 vertical-foot round trip before it gets dark again. Rocky Mountain National Park has two gateways, Estes Park in the east and Grand Lake in the west, with subsidiary parking areas and trailheads at Wild Basin, Longs Peak, Twin Sisters, and Colony Lakes. The densest concentration of hiking trails is on the eastern side of the park.

Sangre de Cristo Wilderness

This huge mountain range east of the Arkansas River Valley and west of the San Luis Valley, includes the best parts of three national forests. Trails from both sides lead to numerous mountain lakes and peaks of 12,000 feet or higher. Lakes of the Clouds and Colony Lakes are among worthy hiking destinations on moderate old roads and trails from the Wet Mountain Valley south of Westcliffe, though the ambitious use them as access to four fourteeners in the stunning Sangre de Cristo Wilderness: Humboldt Peak, Crestone Needle, Crestone Peak, and Kit Carson Peak. Humboldt is the easiest of the bunch, and Crestone Needle the most difficult. Still farther south, two more fourteeners, Blanca Peak and Ellingwood Point, loom over the Huerfano Valley, luring peak baggers, while the mild Huerfano Trail crosses the valley and offers sensational views to casual hikers.

Sawatch Mountains

This range is close to such central Rockies towns as Vail, Eagle, Minturn, and Leadville. The most noteworthy hikes in the northern portion lie in the Holy Cross Wilderness.

Mt. Jackson, Notch Mountain, and Whitney Peak all top 13,000 feet, but the wilderness area's star is the Mount of the Holy Cross. This fourteener was named for the way that snow and ice pack into intersecting couloirs, marking the mountain with a cross of white. The Sawatch extends south toward Leadville and includes a stretch of the Colorado Trail. Holy Cross City, with remnants of a short-lived mining boomtown at 11,500 feet, a grandiose basin holding the Seven Sister Lakes, and Fancy Lake are scenic and interesting day-hike destinations from the Blodgett Campground Trailhead off US 24, halfway between Minturn and Leadville. Fulford Cave is an easy hike from the Fulford Campground Trailhead near Eagle. Enter the cave only if you are knowledgeable about and equipped for underground exploration.

The Sawatch's southern section is notable for Colorado's highest peaks. The big, beefy mountains called Elbert (No. 1 at 14,433 feet) and Massive (No. 2 at 14,421) are considered walk-ups by experienced mountaineers, but their relative ease never can diminish the sense of triumph of being above all the others. Several other 13,000- and 14,000-footers south of Leadville provide wonderful routes and views that are even better. The Collegiate Peaks Wilderness contains a foursome of fourteeners named after Eastern Ivy League universities—Columbia, Harvard, Princeton, and Yale. If you are interested in Colorado's historic train routes, you can hike three easy miles through the Hagerman Tunnel, a standard-gauge railroad tunnel at 11,528 feet.

Uncompahgre Wilderness

The spectacular San Juans, boasting twenty-nine of Colorado's 100 highest peaks and a good chunk of its best scenery, is known as the Switzerland of America. Some half-million wilderness acres in southwestern Colorado comprise Colorado's largest concentration of roadless area, and much of it is as remote as it is magnificent. Of the several wilderness areas, the Uncompahgre Wilderness (until 1993 called the Big Blue Wilderness) stretches between US 550 and State 149 (Lake City Road). Glaciated valleys, spiky peaks, and high, flat tundra make a matchless mix.

American Flats, accessible from the Engineer Pass Road, is a plateau below Wildhorse Peak that is easy as well as spectacular. Though it lies at about 12,500 feet, the hiking is easy (there's a practically flat three-mile trail), affording maximum wildflower-viewing opportunities with minimal strain. American Lake is a lovely destination for the modest yet marvelous trail. Three trails follow three forks of the Cimarron River (East, Middle, and West), each culminating near the wilderness's two fourteeners (Uncompahgre and Wetterhorn) and each offering great scenery. The East and Middle Forks can be combined into a long loop hike.

Upper Rio Grande Valley

The old mining town of Creede, located in a side canyon off the Upper Rio Grande, is surrounded by the La Garita and Weminuche Wilderness areas. Hikers can explore the La Garita Wilderness's western reaches, including trails that follow Martinez Creek and Tumble Creek, as well as a stunning section of the Colorado Trail. Trailheads near the Rio Grande Reservoir, thirty miles west of Creede, enable hikers to penetrate the huge Weminuche Wilderness for day hikes and backpack safaris of various lengths, including to the

13,821-foot summit of a nearly symmetrical peak called the Rio Grande Pyramid. The eighty-mile Continental Divide Trail traverses the Weminuche Wilderness, twice crossing the divide. Trailheads close to Rio Grande Reservoir lead to sections of this compelling trail, much of which is above the timberline. The trail passes a mere 1.5 miles from San Luis Peak, giving stalwart hikers an opportunity to bag an isolated fourteener en route. Creede is also a suitable jumping-off point for hikes into the Wheeler Geologic Area, a 640-acre wonderland of volcanic tuff sculpted and eroded into bizarre and fascinating formations.

But the Creede area is known as much for gentler and more sociable exploration on foot as for its access to gonzo expeditions into remote wilderness areas. A "walking season," from mid-June to October, has been declared by the American Volksport Association, which is dedicated to promoting recreational walking in this country. A series of ten-kilometer summer walks and a fall walk along preestablished trails have been set up. These routes are largely along unpaved roads, and therefore all are relatively easy, with altitude variations from 150 to 1,200 feet; one route is even suitable for walkers pushing wheelchairs or baby strollers. Old mine and mill sites, streams that feed the Rio Grande, and the potential for spotting wildlife await participants. Walkers can get an insignia to attest to their participation in Volksport activities, and "walk bars" for individual events are available. Aspenfest is a one-day event in mid- to late September that is open to AVA members and to the general public. For information, contact:
Upper Rio Grande Mountain Walkers
P.O. Box 272
Creede, CO 81130
800-327-2102, 719-658-2736

West Elk and Raggeds Wilderness Areas

Crested Butte is a charming Victorian town with a contemporary ski resort nearby, but for hikers, it is noteworthy as a convenient base for the surrounding wilderness areas. You can pick short but easy trails like the 2.5-mile Ute Pass Trail, or long but easy trails like the 6.5-mile Oh-Be-Joyful Road leading to Blue Lake. If steep is your desire, try the Daisy Pass Trail or Trail #403 between Washington Gulch and East River. Crested Butte is at the southern end of the Maroon Bells–Snowmass Wilderness, and hikes in the direction of Aspen via a choice of high, scenic passes are among Colorado's top routes. Less widely known wilderness areas are the West Elk Wilderness and Raggeds Wilderness, just west of Crested Butte. The Crested Butte area also lies on the "backside" or west of the Collegiate Peaks Wilderness. The Crested Butte–Mt. Crested Butte Chamber of Commerce (800-545-4505, 970-349-6438) puts out a good overview map of area trails.

TRAIL RUNNING

This is the most gonzo of all the pedestrian activities, combining the stamina of distance running, the skill of mountain hiking, and the willingness to slog through streams, hop over rocks and logs, and continue running through whatever else nature has put on the trail. With its challenging mountain terrain and its population of hard-core fitness fanatics, Colorado is a natural venue for this most demanding outdoor activity.

URBAN HIKES

Walking paths and hiking trails are found in and near cities and towns across the state. A series of free *Colorado Urban Trails Guides* contains maps and updated trail information for four regions: Metro Denver, South Front Range, North Front Range, and Western Slope and Mountains. The Metro Denver publication, for instance, describes 109 trails. A large map of the area shows the trail locations, appropriate uses, level of difficulty, and access for the disabled. The other three map and describe trails near communities elsewhere in Colorado. You can get all four by sending a self-addressed envelope (at least six by nine inches) with six first-class stamps to:
Trail Guides
1313 Sherman Street, Room 618
Denver, CO 80203

Boulder Mountain Parks

Because the city of Boulder butts up against the Rocky Mountain foothills, it has adopted the Flatirons, a distinctive grouping of huge, uptilted rock slabs, as its symbol and inspiration for an urban mountain park system. Time and again, residents have voted to tax themselves for the purchase of open space as a buffer from neighboring communities, and currently the city owns 21,000 acres. Between the mountain parks and the open space along local streams and on the eastern plains, Boulder boasts some of the most diverse open-space environments in the country. Many of the mountain parks' miles of hiking trails can be combined into loops. Because of their relatively low elevation (South Boulder Peak's 8,550-foot summit is the highest), these trails are good in both the early and late seasons, and can serve as a warmup for higher mountains. Still, since many of the trails are steep, they provide a real workout. The Mesa Trail, skirting the foothills and passing close to the base of the Flatirons, is six miles long with an elevation variation of just 600 feet and provides a grand overview of Boulder and its unsurpassed parks. Rangers lead free nature hikes in the mountain parks on Saturdays in June and July, starting at the Chautauqua Park Ranger Cottage.

Cherry Creek State Park

Located ten miles southeast of Denver, this popular park, abutting Cherry Creek Reservoir, combines urban (or at least suburban) convenience with the expansive elbow-room of the plains. While it is best known for the water sports the reservoir encourages, it also boasts hiking trails suitable for a leisurely stroll or a vigorous run.

Garden of the Gods

The Garden of the Gods is the perfect counterpoint to the touristic overload of Colorado Springs, which has the most commercial attractions in the state. The Garden of the Gods, a 1,350-acre park below Pikes Peak, boasts miles of trails winding among red sandstone formations that are positively sculptural. Balanced Rock and Steamboat Rock are the two most famous and most photographed formations, but numerous others are compelling as well.

GUIDED HIKES AND NATURE WALKS

Guided hikes combine security and information on the geology, flora, fauna, and history of a region. The guide is often a trained wildlife biologist who is also knowledgeable about the backcountry and trained in first aid. In addition to offering regularly scheduled hikes, most guides can customize an itinerary according to participants' interests and energy.

GUIDE SERVICES, HIKES, AND WALKS

Aspen Alpine Guides
P.O. Box 659
Aspen, CO 81612
970-925-6618
Elk Mountains

Aspen Center for Environmental Studies (ACES)
P.O. Box 8777
Aspen, CO 81612
970-925-5756
Nature walks and interpretative hikes in the Aspen area

Blazing Trails
55 East Durant
Aspen, CO 81611
800-282-7238, 970-925-5651 (Aspen), 970-923-4544
    (Snowmass)
Elk Mountains

Elk Mountain Guides
P.O. Box 10327
Aspen, CO 8162
970-927-9377
Elk Mountains; history of Ashcroft hike; guided hikes to selected fourteeners

Fantasy Ridge Mountain Guides
P.O. Box 1679
Telluride, CO 81435
970-728-3546
San Juans

Herb Walker Tours
P.O. Box 399
Telluride, CO 81435
970-728-4538
Herb and plant walks near town and in the high country

Lizard Head Mountain Guides
P.O. Box 1560
150 West Colorado Avenue
Telluride, CO 81435
800-828-7547, 970-728-4904
San Juans

Paragon Guides
P.O. Box 130
Vail, CO 81658
970-926-5299
White River National Forest, including Mount of the Holy Cross; Mt. Massive and Mt. Elbert summit climbs

Sawatch Naturalists and Guides
P.O. Box 53
Leadville, CO 80461
719-486-1856
San Isabel National Forest; naturalist walks and hikes

Shrine Mountain Adventure
P.O. Box 4
Red Cliff, CO 81649
970-827-5363
White River National Forest (near Vail) nature hikes; summit
hikes to Notch Mountain and Galena Mountain in the Holy
Cross Wilderness

Southwest Adventures
P.O. Box 3242
Durango, CO 81302
800-642-5389, 970-259-0370
San Juan Mountains

COLORADO MOUNTAIN CLUB

The Colorado Mountain Club, a membership organization,
is a treasure trove of information on Colorado's hikes.
In addition to the main clubhouse in Golden, just west of
Denver, nineteen other clubhouses are in major cities and
towns throughout Colorado's mountain region. All have
extensive resources, including guidebooks. Other services
include mountaineering courses, informative slide shows,
equipment trade-ins, and summit registers for notable
mountaintops so that all those who reach the top can

document their accomplishment. Volunteers also lead hikes throughout the year, and visiting nonmembers may join at the leader's option and on a space-available basis.

Colorado Mountain Club
710 Tenth Street
Golden, CO 80401
303-279-3080

DOWNHILL HIKES

To get the best of the scenery and the wildflowers without defying gravity, buy a ticket at one of the ski areas that has a lift for sightseeing and/or mountain biking, and then just walk down. (See the "Pedal Power" chapter.) In addition to the Aspen Institute for Environmental Studies' guided nature walks from the top of Aspen Mountain (see above), guided area nature walks are available from lift-served areas on Vail Mountain and Copper Mountain.

HIKES FOR THE HANDICAPPED

Wheelchair-accessible trails, smooth barrier-free walkways, and interpretive trails for blind and visually impaired visitors are being developed across Colorado. In many instances, special efforts have been made to route even the shortest of these trails through varying ecosystems and/or to points with outstanding views. While these can hardly be misrepresented as "hikes" or "backcountry adventures," at least they are opening these activities to disabled people.

LOCATION, LENGTH, SURFACE, AND OTHER NOTES

Alamosa Wildlife Refuge
3 miles southeast of Alamosa
719-589-2271
2 miles; hardpacked service road; wheelchair accessible
except during wet conditions; open March 1 to November 1

Big L
Mancos, U.S. 160 west of Durango
970-533-7716
.5 mile; hardened gravel; gentle climb; benches every 400
feet

Can Do Trail
McPhee Reservoir, north of Cortez
970-882-7296
1 mile; hardened gravel; considered difficult for wheelchairs; benches along trail

Chatfield State Park (fee area)
Southwest Littleton
303-791-7275
11 miles; paved, including route to heron rookery (guided
tours available each May)

Glenwood Canyon Path
East of Glenwood Springs
970-945-6589
18 miles; paved (heavily traveled by cyclists, runners,
and walkers)

Living Waters Interpretive Center
Belmar Park, Lakewood
303-987-7850
.8 mile; crusher fines; boardwalk

Ridgway State Park (fee area)
Montrose
970-626-5822
5 miles; half paved, half gravel

Rocky Mountain National Park
970-586-1206,
970-586-1319 (V/TDD)
Beaver Ponds Boardwalk, .25 mile
Coyote Valley Boardwalk, .5 mile
Sprague Lake Trail, 1 mile; compacted earth

Roaring Fork Braille Trail
State 82, east of Aspen
970-925-3445
.25 mile; natural surface; 22 stations with Braille signs

South Mesa Trail
Eldorado Springs Road, south of Boulder
303-441-4142
.25 mile; crusher fines

Spring Creek Mountain Park
Steamboat Springs
970-879-2060
.4 mile; crusher fines

Stapleton Park Nature Trail
Stapleton Park, Lookout Mountain
303-697-4545
.6 mile; natural surface (not suitable for wheelchairs);
Braille signs

Summit Lake Tundra Trail
Mt. Evans, south of Idaho Springs
303-964-2500
.3 mile; crusher fines

Walter Orr Roberts Nature Trail
National Center for Atmospheric Research, west of Boulder
303-497-1174
.3 mile; crusher fines; moderate grade; may require assis-
tance for wheelchairs

Williams Fork Boardwalk
Dillon
970-724-9004
1,800 feet

Winter Park Outdoor Center
Winter Park Ski Area
970-892-0961,
970-892-0961 (V/TDD)
1.25 miles; crusher fines; two boardwalks, compacted
earth; one climbing trail for sport wheelchairs; picnic tables
with overhangs for wheelchairs

Some outfitters and guide services are particular sensitive to the needs of the mobility-impaired, among them Sawtooth Naturalists & Guides (see section on "Guided Hikes and Nature Walks").

TIPS FOR HIKERS

Hiking is reason enough to visit Colorado. The scenery is breathtaking and the opportunity to explore wild areas is thrilling. The hiking season begins in late spring, which means after Memorial Day for high mountains and/or in heavy snow years, and winds down in October, when the snow again begins to blanket the high country. But hiking in Colorado is not to be taken lightly or without adequate preparation any time of the year. The mountains' splendor is matched only by the capriciousness of the weather.

Even midsummer hikers bound for high elevations should be prepared for rain or wintry weather, and lightning is a real hazard. Hiking in Colorado demands preparation and precautions in order to maximize the fabulous experience and minimize the risks. It is prudent never to hike alone, but if you are fit and experienced, at least let someone know where you are going and when you expect to return—and stick to the program. Colorado newspapers frequently publish news about "lost hikers," and while most are eventually found safe, some are not.

With trailheads at 8,000 feet or more above sea level, Colorado's mountains are high and dry, so they require every hiker to be aware of potential hazards. The altitude can cause shortness of breath, dizziness, or even altitude sickness, especially nonacclimated visitors. The best advice is to spend a day or two in Denver or another Front Range city to begin adjusting to the altitude, to take it easy (walking uphill steadily like a tortoise is better than hare-like sprint-and-stop hiking), and to drink more water than you think you need.

Colorado mornings tend to be glorious, with blue skies and brilliant sunshine that most people think are the fiction of postcards and tourist brochures. Frequently, however, clouds begin to build late in summer mornings, and squally rain showers and even bursts of snow or hail are common in the afternoons, especially at high altitudes. The first rule is to start hiking early and quit early. Especially for long hikes with great elevation gains, hikers should start shortly after sunrise and be prepared to turn around and try again another day if they don't reach their goal by noon.

Lightning is not just a great light show. It is potentially lethal, and above the timberline there are few places to hide. If you are in the mountains when storms seem to be moving in, descend from high points. If you cannot get away from an exposed area, make yourself as small as possible by crouching down and balancing on the balls of your feet or by sitting on a small rock with insulation, such as a poncho or foam pad, under you, with your feet touching the rock and your hands clasped around your knees. Never seek shelter under a lone tree, in a shallow cave, or under a rock overhang.

It is best not to smoke at all in the backcountry, but if you must, smother your cigarette and carry out the butts. Cigarette filters, while small, are pervasive litter because they decompose slowly. Finally, to protect the fragile wilderness, stay on the trail. Short-cutting causes erosion.

What to Bring

Water, water, water must be the first item on any hiker's list. Because the climate is dry—and the hotter the temperature, the drier it will most likely be—take at least a pint per person for a very short hike, and a quart or more per person for a longer one, such as a half-day summer hike with significant elevation gain or a full-day hike that is relatively flat. A strenuous, full-day hike requires at least two quarts per person. Better to have too much water than too little. It's a good idea to pack as much ice into each water bottle as it will hold and fill water around it, so that you'll be drinking cold or cool water as long as possible.

Minimum equipment, even for a short hike, includes sunscreen, sunglasses, hat, and hiking boots or sturdy shoes with good soles (plus adhesive bandages or moleskin, unless both the footwear and the feet are well broken in). If you're planning to hike several miles and reach altitudes of up to 10,000 feet, it's a good idea to carry a fleece jacket or wool sweater and windshirt. An energy boosting snack is usually welcome along the way. For multi-milers and elevation gains above 10,000 feet (and especially above the timberline), it is advisable to bring long johns, rain gear, a warm hat, gloves, an emergency blanket, and extra food. For strenuous hikes above the timberline involving snow crossings or scree, an ice ax can be useful, but only if you know how to use it.

It's hard to get lost on well-trafficked, well-marked trails at low elevations, but a map and a good guidebook are helpful anyway, if just to orient you and clue you in about what you are seeing. In remote areas and at higher elevations, these aids are essential, as are a good topographical map, a compass, an altimeter, a Swiss army knife, matches in a waterproof case, and even a flashlight in case you're on the trail longer than expected or are injured and need to signal for help.

What Not to Bring

Flimsy shoes, handbags, valuables, and constricting clothing top the leave-behind list. In some places, including the national parks, dogs are not permitted; on public lands where they are allowed, they must be under reliable voice command or on a leash.

An excellent booklet called *Recreational Survival Guide* is issued by Mountain Rescue–Aspen, Inc., 630 West Main Street, Aspen, CO 81611; 970-925-7172. It's free, but this organization, like others that provide backcountry rescue, welcomes donations.

HOW YOU CAN HELP

Volunteers for Outdoor Colorado is a nonprofit organization. Since its inception in 1984, VOC has enlisted over 16,000 volunteers and completed more than sixty-nine outdoor work projects with an estimated improvement value approaching $3 million. You can register for summer projects by calling VOC, which will assign you to an experienced crew leader and provide instructions about where and when to arrive, what to bring, what the camping arrangements or overnight-lodging options are, and what meals and equipment VOC will provide. Some projects are suitable for families with children as young as eight.

Volunteers for Outdoor Colorado
410 Grant Street, Suite B-105
Denver, CO 80203
303-830-7792

READING LIST

The Best of Colorado Hiking Trails by Don and Roberta
   Lowe (Outdoor Books & Maps, P.O. Box 417, Denver,
   CO 80201)

Best Hikes with Children in Colorado by Maureen Keilty
   (The Mountaineers, 1011 S.W. Klickitat Way, Seattle,
   WA 98134)

A Climbing Guide to Colorado's Fourteeners by Walter R.
   Borneman and Lyndon J. Lampert (Pruett Publishing
   Co., 2928 Pearl Street, Boulder, CO 80301)

Colorado's BLM Wilderness: Hiking & Floating by Mark
   Pearson & John Fielder (Westcliffe Publishers, Inc.,
   2650 South Zuni Street, Englewood, CO 80110)

Colorado's Continental Divide by Ron Ruhoff (Cordillera
   Press, P.O. Box 3699, Evergreen, CO 80439)

Colorado's Fourteeners by Gary Roach (Fulcrum Publishing, 350 Indiana Street, Golden, CO 80401)

Colorado Fourteeners Grand Slam by Roger Edrinn (Above
   the Timber, 2366 Wapiti Road, Fort Collins, CO 80525)

Colorado's High Thirteeners by Mike Garrett and Bob
   Martin (Cordillera Press)

Colorado Mountain Hikes for Everyone by Dave Muller
   (Quality Press, DJM Enterprises, P.O. Box 61332,
   Denver, CO 80206)

Colorado Mountain Hikes and Ski Tours by Dave Muller
   (Quality Press)

Colorado Mountains edited by Randy Jacobs (Colorado Mountain Club, 710 Tenth Street, Golden, CO 80401)

Colorado Wildlife Viewing Guide by Mary Taylor Gray (Falcon Books, P.O. Box 1718, Helena, MT 59624)

Colorado on Foot by Robert L. Brown (Caxton Printers, Caldwell, ID 83605)

Colorado's Other Mountains by Walter R. Borneman (Cordillera Press)

Dawson's Guide to Colorado's Fourteeners by Louis W. Dawson II (Blue Clover Press, 19650 Blue Clover Lane, Monument, CO 81032)

Day Hikes on the Colorado Trail by Janet Robertson (American Traveler Guidebooks, 541 Oak Street, P.O. Box 177, Frederick, CO 80534; Colorado Trail Foundation, P.O. Box 260876, Lakewood, CO 80226)

Ecology of Western Forests by John C. Kircher and Gordon Morrison (Houghton Mifflin, 2 Park Street, Boston, MA 02108)

Exploring Colorado's Wilderness Areas by Scott S. Warren (The Mountaineers)

500 Short Hikes in Colorado's High and Low Country for the Average Hiker by G. V. and Vivian Douglas (Douglas & Douglas, Inc., P.O. Box 6188, Battlement Mesa, CO 81636)

The Hiker's Guide to Colorado by Doug Wheat (Falcon Books)

Hiking the Highest Passes by Bob Martin (Pruett Publishing)

Rocky Mountain Walks by Gary Ferguson (Fulcrum Publishing)

Uphill Both Ways by Robert L. Brown (Caxton Printers)

Pruett also publishes a series of Colorado regional hiking guides: *Hiking Trails of Southwestern Colorado* by Paul Pixler, *Hiking Trails of Northern Colorado* by Mary

Hagen, *Hiking Trails of Central Colorado* by Bob Martin, *Hiking Trails of the Boulder Mountain Parks and Plains* by Vici de Haan, *The South San Juan Wilderness Area* by John Murray, and *Hiking Guide to the Mount Zirkel Wilderness Area* by Jay and Therese Thompson.

7

OUT FOR THE NIGHT

If you like to hike, you'll love multi-day excursions, which are the natural next step after one-day trips.. A longer trek provides the opportunity to explore an area in depth or to cover many miles and really see and feel the high country, to study the wildflowers, photograph the scenery, and generally steep yourself in the beauty and tranquillity of the mountains. Multi-day hiking, by definition, means camping, and several options fall into that broad category.

TYPES OF CAMPING

Colorado boasts more than 30,000 campsites scattered throughout deep forests, high on mountainsides, beside rivers or lakes, and even in the outskirts of larger cities, as well as in untold backcountry acres where wilderness camping prevails. The choice of how and where to camp is a function of style, budget, and availability of the selected site. To narrow down the choices, consider why you want to camp and how rugged you want your experience to be. There's something of a tradeoff, with comforts, conveniences, and accessibility being in inverse proportion to the remoteness, privacy, and scenic qualities of a campsite.

First, for maximum ease but minimum flexibility, you can drive into a roadside campground with a tent, trailer, or motor home and use it as a base for day hikes. If you decide on a developed campground, you have a second choice, between a commercial campground and one on public land. All have sanitary facilities, picnic tables, and grills, but private campgrounds generally have utility hookups (electricity, water, and sewerage), showers, laundry, grocery, playground, and other such conveniences. Electricity brings with it televisions, stereos, brighter lights, and other "conveniences" that, to most tent campers, destroy any feeling of "wilderness" and "outdoors." To others, like RVers, this degree of comfort is necessary to make the wilderness less wild, the outdoors less out, and the whole notion of camping palatable. For families or older campers, such conveniences are often necessary.

To extend your range afoot, you must graduate to longer hikes, which you can do in several ways, including the third camping option—backpacking to a primitive campsite. Campsites may be assigned on a permit basis or may be first come, first served.

The fourth option is for you if, and only if, you are well-equipped and totally comfortable in the wilderness. Then you can find a spot to camp within whatever zones park or forest managers have established for at-large camping. A zone system sets a quota for the maximum number of campers permitted in a given place, such as a valley or a lakeshore, but allows campers to pitch tents anywhere within it. In heavily used sections, park and forest managers occasionally designate sites to concentrate use and avoid excessive damage, in essence a hybrid between a primitive campsite and zone-system camping.

The final option is to carry a pack and food but sleep in a hut or perhaps a yurt, which for some people is the ideal combination of rugged hiking and civilized eating and sleeping. Many mountaineering stores rent equipment such as tents, packs, and sleeping bags.

Backpacking also can be an end unto itself, a chance to steep oneself in the majesty of the mountains and, on a very rudimentary level, test one's ability to survive, or it can be a means to achieve other goals, such as backpacking to a base for mountain climbing or fishing. You must choose whether to hike independently or as part of an organized group. All the pros and cons of guided day hikes apply to excursions of several days—multiplied. The benefits of guided excursions include appropriate equipment, organization, security, and companionship. Some outfitters schedule special treks for singles, which is the only sensible approach to the backcountry for the solo traveler who is not totally at home in the wilderness. The biggest drawback is the cost, which can seem high for an experience that, after all, is supposed to be low-key and low-cost, but, if you are on your own, you have to decide how, when, and where to camp. On a paid excursion, there's always space in the hut or campsite.

Each style of camping carries with it different requirements in terms of equipment, energy, cost, expenditure, and advance planning. See the "Afoot" chapter for a primer on the state's geography, mountain life zones, and most popular hiking areas. These and more are suitable for camping. See Appendix for a list of government agencies that operate public campgrounds and issue permits for backcountry camping.

CAMPING IN FEDERAL LANDS

NATIONAL PARKS AND NATIONAL MONUMENTS

MESA VERDE NATIONAL PARK

Campgrounds

Morefield Village Campground is a fully equipped overnight facility with groceries, showers, laundromat, and other services. It is open from May to mid-October.

ROCKY MOUNTAIN NATIONAL PARK

Campgrounds

The snow-capped peaks and high tundra give this spectacular park its appeal, but the five campgrounds within park boundaries are at much lower elevations in a more benign climatic zone. All are easily accessible to vehicles and are fee areas, but none offers hookups or showers. Moraine Park and Glacier Basin, both on the east (or Estes Park) side, operate on an advance reservation system (800-365-CAMP), while Longs Peak Campground and Aspenglen Campground, both also on the east side, and Timber Creek Campground on the west (or Grand Lake) side are first come, first served. Longs Peak is only for tents. Camping is limited to seven nights from June 1 through September 30 (three nights for Longs Peak).

Backpacking

Although the backcountry is what makes Rocky Mountain National Park so special for people, heavy pressure has mandated rather stringent rules. Backcountry permits are required for overnights and are issued for a specific location and specific date, with a maximum of seven nights (three nights at any one campsite) between May and September and fifteen nights the rest of the year. Wood or charcoal fires are permitted only in the few sites with fire rings. A limited number of permits are also issued for camping in so-called cross-country zones, which have no developed trails or campsites. All permits require campsites to be below the timberline, at least 100 feet from a water source, out of sight and sound of any other party, and moved at least one mile each day. Reservations for permits for backcountry campsites or cross-country camping must be made in person at the backcountry offices adjacent to the Park Headquarters on the Estes Park side or the Kawuneeche visitors center on the Grand Lake side, or in writing to: Backcountry Office, Rocky Mountain National Park, Estes Park, CO 80517. No phone reservations are taken, but for information, call 970-586-4459.

BLACK CANYON OF THE GUNNISON NATIONAL MONUMENT

Campgrounds

There may be deeper and narrower canyons, but the Black combines depth, narrowness, and sheer rock walls in a proportion unmatched anywhere else. This twelve-mile-long gorge, etched by the Gunnison River, is frequently mentioned as a future national park and has long been nicknamed Colorado's Grand Canyon. The steep and deep chasm is especially noteworthy as a habitat for cliff-dwelling birds. The South Rim Campground is the largest facility, and each campsite there has a table and either fireplace or charcoal grill. East Portal and North Rim Campgrounds are smaller, but all are fee areas, operated on a first-come, first-served basis.

Backpacking

A handful of campsites are located off popular hiking trails and along the Gunnison River.

Black Canyon of the Gunnison
2233 East Main Street
Montrose, CO 81401
970-249-7036

COLORADO NATIONAL MONUMENT

Campgrounds

Colorado National Monument is the heart of the Colorado Plateau, rising 2,000 feet above the Grand Valley of the Colorado River. Its brilliant landscape is a maze of huge plateaus and river-carved canyons that epitomize the West. Remote and bold, the area is known for its abundant wildlife, splendid photographic opportunities, and the perspective brought by humbling scale and wide horizons. Saddlehorn Campground, located in a forest of scrub pinion and juniper near the visitors center, has first-come, first-served campsites with table, charcoal grill, and access to restrooms and water. A fee is charged from April through October, but camping is free the rest of the year.

Backpacking

Backcountry camping is allowed anywhere more than one-quarter mile from roads and 100 yards from trails. There is no formal permit system, but backpackers are asked to register at the visitors' center.

Colorado National Monument
Fruita, CO 81521
970-858-3617

DINOSAUR NATIONAL MONUMENT

Campgrounds

In the dim past, what is now a bone-dry desert was a sea and later a marsh where dinosaurs and other creatures roamed, leaving fossils as reminders of the ancient past. Other reminders are the petroglyphs drawn by the Fremont people on canyon walls as evidence of their presence. More recent visitors to the area were fur trader William H. Ashley, who floated the Green River in 1825, and explorer John Wesley Powell, who did so in 1869.

Today, campers stake their claims to sites at Split

Mountain Campground and Green River Campground, the most developed facilities in the area. Both charge a fee and accomodate RVs. Deerlodge Campground above the Yampa River Canyon, Echo Park Campground at the confluence of the Green and Yampa Rivers, Gates of Lodore Campground above Lodore Canyon on the Green, and Rainbow Park Campground on the Green are primitive, no-fee facilities. Some are accessible by four-wheel drive and other sturdy vehicles, but not recommended for RVs. Water availability is uneven. Check with the superintendent.

Backpacking

There are few trails in this canyon-laced, high-desert monument to Colorado's prehistory, so the few backpackers who hike in share campgrounds with rafters pulling off the river for the night. Dry and rugged are the best words to describe the conditions backpackers will encounter. Since the designated campgrounds are really basic, camping there and day hiking is a viable alternative to backpacking.

Dinosaur National Monument
P.O. Box 210
4545 U.S. 40
Dinosaur, CO 81610
970-374-2216

HOVENWEEP NATIONAL MONUMENT

Campgrounds

This Anasazi showcase, a neighbor both spiritually and physically to Mesa Verde National Park, has one campground near Square Tower Ruins. A fee is charged.

Mesa Verde National Park
Mesa Verde National Park, CO 81330
970-529-4465

GREAT SAND DUNES NATIONAL MONUMENT

Backpacking

Camping is allowed in the Great Sand Dunes National Monument. No fee is charged and no permit is required, but backpackers are asked to register at the visitors' center.

Great Sand Dunes National Monument
11999 Colorado State Highway 150
Mosca, CO 81146
719-378-2312

NATIONAL FORESTS

Campgrounds

The vast national forest lands of Colorado are dotted with drive-in campgrounds large and small, and the U.S. Forest Service (USFS) also handles National Recreation Area campgrounds. Drive-in campgrounds are set up for tents and for trailers and RVs up to thirty feet long. Facilities are basic—generally designated sites with fireplace or fire ring and perhaps with picnic tables, privies, and running water.

Most campgrounds are open from Memorial Day through Labor Day. Where they are accessible in the off-season, there is usually no water, and users are asked to take trash out with them.

Usually, only campgrounds with running water charge fees. These are collected on site and generally are $5 to $10 per day. Stays are normally limited to fourteen days, less at some locations. The USFS's annually updated flyer, *Rocky Mountain Region Campgrounds*, lists national forests and ranger districts with phone numbers and the names of developed campgrounds, number of spaces, and nightly fees (if any). It is available from USFS offices or by calling 800-280-CAMP, or 800-879-4496 for the hearing-impaired.

Backpacking

Backcountry camping is free, but other policies differ from forest to forest, season to season, and may depend on current use patterns. In general, camping is permitted anywhere in a national forest or wilderness area except where specifically prohibited. Permit requirements vary. Individual USFS offices, listed in the Appendix, can provide information and maps.

CURECANTI NATIONAL RECREATION AREA

Campgrounds

This recreation area, whose centerpiece is the twenty-mile-long Blue Mesa Lake, was created by three dams on the Gunnison River. It is a place of stark beauty, where the deep water contrasts with canyons and mesas, sheer cliffs, and rock spires. Cimarron, an area best known for excellent fishing and boating, offers excellent hiking trails and wildlife viewing as well. Cimarron, Elk Creek, Lake Fork, and Stevens Creek are the most developed campgrounds. Dry Gulch, Gateview, Ponderosa, and Red Creek are less developed and more secluded. All are first-come, first-served fee areas. Only East Elk Creek Group Campground requires reservations; call 970-641-2337.

Backpacking

Camping is permitted only in designated sites, but Curecanti is more suited for short backpacks or for introductory experiences for families than for rugged backcountry experiences.

CAMPING IN STATE LANDS

STATE PARKS

Colorado's forty state parks, comprising some of the state's most diverse and breathtaking scenery, are among the unheralded wonders of the Rocky Mountain region. Stretching from Sterling in the northeast to Mancos in the southwest, from Steamboat/Pearl near the Wyoming border to Trinidad near New Mexico, these natural lands offer splendid camping. The developed campgrounds offer 300 sites for RVs and tents and frequently feature amenities such as a visitors service center, electrical hookups, flush restrooms, and showers. Fees vary and are slightly higher for sites with hookups. Twenty-eight areas offer primitive campsites with fire rings, grills, and picnic tables, and authentic backcountry camping for backpackers is available in some parks. The Campground Reservations Office handles bookings for all state parks: 800-678-2267, 303-470-1140.

A free guide to campgrounds and other recreational facilities in these parks is available from:
Colorado State Parks
1313 Sherman Street, Suite 618
Denver, CO 80303
303-866-3437

COLORADO STATE FOREST

Campgrounds

Stretching between the Never Summer Range and the Medicine Bow Mountains in northern Colorado, this forest epitomizes the state's high country—if not its highest country. It has no fourteeners and no thirteeners either, but the 70,000 acres of montane and sub-Alpine forest lands provide excellent camping, fishing, boating, hiking, horseback riding, biking, and four-wheeling. Bochman, The Crags, North Michigan Reservoir, and Ranger Lakes campgrounds have designated sites for tents, trailers, and campers. There is a fee to enter the state forest, and a camping permit is also required.

Backpacking

Ruby Lake, Kelly Lake, Clear Lake, and American Lake have been designated as backcountry campsites. Register with the ranger.

Colorado State Forest
Star Route 91
Walden, CO 80480
970-723-8366

BACKPACKING TRAILS

THE COLORADO TRAIL

The 470-mile Colorado Trail between Waterton Canyon, near Chatfield Reservoir southwest of Denver, and Durango, in southwestern Colorado, is one of only a few national trails built by volunteers to provide access to areas of special interest. It traverses some of the most beautiful terrain in the state, including Summit County's high peaks, the historic mining towns of Leadville and Creede, the Collegiate Peaks Wilderness, Alpine crests on the Continental Divide, and the San Juan Mountains between Silverton and Durango. En route, it passes through seven national forests, eight mountain ranges, five major river systems, and six wilderness areas. Novice or sometime hikers can enjoy walks as short as a mile, while experts with time and stamina can do the entire trail, perhaps over several summers.

A must-have guidebook documents the trail's history and development, a brief description of the geology and natural environments, and practical information on hiking the trail, including campsites, access points, and distances. Another covers suggested day hikes along the trail. Both are available from the Colorado Trail Foundation (see the reading list at the end of this chapter). A map series with detailed topographical information, including trailheads,

151

parking areas, and nearby towns, is a necessary supplement for anyone contemplating hiking the trail.

Colorado Trail Foundation
P.O. Box 260876
Lakewood, CO 80226
303-986-4351

CONTINENTAL DIVIDE TRAIL

Stretching eighty astonishingly scenic miles through the Weminuche Wilderness between Stony Pass and Wolf Creek Pass, this challenging trail offers incredible views and most likely solitude. Much of the trail is along the timberline, making it suitable only for strong, experienced backpackers prepared to deal with high altitude and Colorado's squirrelly summer weather. The wildflowers bloom in unsurpassed profusion during the short summer (a hike planned anytime after mid-September is an invitation to winter camping), and several stunning mountain ranges provide a succession of magnificent bakcdrops.

GORE RANGE TRAIL

This 54.5-mile trail is so named because it offers wonderful views of the jagged Gore Range, not because it is in the range. All nine trailheads are within two hours' drive from Denver. The route passes numerous lakes and streams in both the Arapaho and White River National Forests, with the most spectacular stretches skirting the Eagles Nest

Wilderness. This trail—one of just two crossing the entire wilderness area—is a particularly valued backcountry treasure because it is a close neighbor of the highly developed resorts of the Vail Valley and Summit County.

HIGH LONESOME

This trail just below the crest of the Continental Divide offers extraordinary scenery and access to the highest summits and passes of the Indian Peaks Wilderness, the most splendid part of Roosevelt National Forest. With its exceptional proximity to Denver/Boulder, and its easy combinability with Rocky Mountain National Park, High Lonesome can be done in segments. Although the trailheads are among Colorado's most used, the high trail merits its name, and if you backpack it, you'll encounter few other hikers. Access from the west is the Monarch Lake Trailhead near Granby or the Devil's Thumb Park Trailhead near Fraser. Access from the east is the Hessie Trailhead near Nederland.

WYOMING TRAIL

Stretching forty miles from Buffalo Pass near Steamboat Springs into Medicine Bow National Forest across the Wyoming state line, this often remote and sometimes indistinct trail winds through ranching country, where you may encounter livestock, and the Mt. Zirkel Wilderness, where you probably will encounter wildlife. The views into North Park and the Yampa Valley are among northern Colorado's best, and it's a toss-up whether summer's wildflowers or autumn's golden aspens are better.

AMERICAN DISCOVERY TRAIL

In 1969, the American Hiking Society spearheaded the creation of America's first nonmotorized coast-to-coast hiking trail, linking cities and traversing mountain wildernesses, forests, and deserts. From Utah in the west, the Colorado section crosses Colorado National Monument, Grand Mesa, Schofield Pass, Crested Butte, the Colorado Trail's Continental Divide section, Evergreen, Colorado Springs, Cañon City, and the high plains to Lamar, and on to the Kansas border in the east.

American Discovery Trail
1046 Azalea Court
Virginia Beach, VA 23452
800-851-3442

HUT AND YURT OVERNIGHTS

The Tenth Mountain Division huts, developed for ski touring, are open in summer for hiking and mountain biking with specific hiking trails between some of them but roads shared with four-wheel-drive vehicles and mountain bikes between others. As the popularity of "off-season" use of huts grows, more systems will be staying open in summer or are seeking U.S. Forest Service permission to do so. Some may cater exclusively to guided groups, while others are open to individuals as well. See the "Over the Snow" chapter for systems; you must call to check on the current status of each of them.

COMMERCIAL CAMPGROUNDS

Purists would never describe most private campgrounds, some of which have swimming pools and even some cabins for rent, as relating any more to the outdoors than a trailer park or a motel does. Yet their popularity indicates that this balance of comfort and access to outdoor pursuits is appropriate for many people. Some campgrounds offer especially good access to fishing, hiking, or other outdoor activities, and for winter travelers, a few are open year-round. Some campgrounds are only for RVs and trailers, but most also have tent spaces. A free directory, including facilities, number of spaces, and fees, is available from:
Colorado Association of Campgrounds, Cabins, and Lodges
5101 Pennsylvania Avenue
Boulder, CO 80303
303-499-9343

GUIDED OVERNIGHT HIKES

In addition to the outfitters below, see the "Horsepower" chapter for horsepacking and llama outfitters offering overnight excursions.

OUTFITTERS AND HIKES

Elk Mountain Guides
P.O. Box 10327
Aspen, CO 81612
970-927-9377
Elk Mountains

Paragon Guides
P.O. Box 130
Vail, CO 81658
970-926-5299
Tenth Mountain Trail hut trips

Roads Less Traveled
P.O. Box 8187
Longmont, CO 80501
303-678-8750
Rocky Mountain National Park, hut trips; specializes in hike-and-bike combinations

Trail Skills
2696 West U.S. 160
Monte Vista, CO 81144
719-852-3277
Backpack excursions to Wheeler Geologic Area, Rio Grande National Forest

CAMPING FOR THE HANDICAPPED

The following public-land camping facilities offer wheel-chair-accessible campsites and restrooms or privies. Also check private campgrounds, which are often more developed and therefore also accessible to disabled campers.

Big L
Mancos
970-533-7716

Curecanti National Recreation Area
Between Gunnison and Montrose
970-641-2337

Handi Camp
Rocky Mountain National Park
970-586-4459

South Rim Campground
Black Canyon of the Gunnison National Monument
970-249-7036

Winter Park Outdoor Center
Winter Park
970-892-0961

TIPS FOR CAMPERS

The New Wilderness Ethic

If you still carry with you the image of scouts hacking their way through the forest, digging a fire pit, and stoking the campfire with any chunk of wood they could chop or find, retire it. The new wilderness ethic, which should apply anywhere in life but does especially to backcountry camping, is "Pack it in; pack it out," and its corollary, "Take nothing but pictures, leave nothing but footprints." Because of Colorado's elevation and dry climate, damage to soil, plants, and water sources is rapid, and recovery takes a long time. Backpackers need to be even more vigilant than

157

casual day hikers. Camping practices that leave no traces of use are the highest form of backcountry camping.

Try to find a secondhand campsite to avoid unnecessarily stressing the natural environment. Signs of previous use include spots where vegetation is worn away and a fire ring exists. The only man-made structure to leave in the backcountry is a fire ring. In many cases, there are established policies for fire (often no open fires) or distance from water sources that must be maintained. Where it is impossible to camp in a "used" spot, be especially gentle with the wilderness. Whether you pitch your tent in a developed campsite or in the pristine wilderness, leave your site as clean as you found it—or better.

Colorado is no longer considered grizzly country, but you wouldn't want to chance sharing your food cache with a hungry black bear, so pack food or trash in bags and suspend them from high lines strung between trees that are away from your campsite.

Sanitation

Human waste and toilet paper must be disposed of properly. Use a small trowel to dig a "cat hole" six to eight inches deep, at least 200 feet from any water source, and bury human waste. Toilet paper can be burned. (No one likes cigarettes in the backcountry but a lighter is useful for this.) If, and only if, the ground is truly too hard to dig, build a rock cairn over the waste pile to keep animals away. Normal soaps and detergents introduce unnatural chemicals into the environment. Instead, use hot water, elbow grease, and special soaps that are available in camping stores to minimize damage. Still, wash yourself and utensils with as little soap and water as possible and do these chores away from streams and lakes.

Drinking Water

It is possible to carry enough water for day hiking, but for a backpacking trip, it's nearly impossible. As clear as Colorado's mountains streams appear, they can carry a parasite called giardia, which causes flu-like symptoms and damage to the digestive system that can persist. Water must be boiled, treated with iodine, or pumped through a special filter to remove the menacing little beast.

What to Bring

Bring everything that's on the list in the Afoot chapter, plus camping gear and a strong, comfortable backpack. Equipment needs include a tent (extra pegs are a good idea), ground cloth, sponge or brush to keep the tent clean when breaking camp, foam or an inflatable pad, sleeping bag, camp stove, fuel, matches in a waterproof case, cooking and eating utensils, pot scrubber, towel, toilet paper, food in spillproof containers or sealed plastic bags, plastic trash bag, extra water containers, water filter or iodine, headlamp and/or flashlight with functioning batteries, first-aid kit, insect repellent, sneakers or other camp footwear, enough clothing for any kind of weather, custom orthotics for your boots, walking stick, camp chair, lantern, portable shower, and clothesline.

What Not to Bring

Just about anything goes in some commercial campgrounds, or so it seems, but the backcountry ethic is different. Leave behind loud radios, cellular phones, and other
urban trappings, and, in certain areas such as national
parks or anywhere at all if you hope to see any wildlife, the
family dog.

READING LIST

Colorado RV Parks—A Pictorial Guide by Hilton and Jenny
Fitt-Peaster (Rocky Mountain Vacation Publishing, 5101
Pennsylvania Avenue, Boulder, CO 80303)

The Complete Colorado Campground Guide edited by Jack
O. Olofson (Outdoor Books, P.O. Box 24, Denver, CO
80201)

The Complete Guide to Rocky Mountain Camping by Tom
Stienstra (Foghorn Press, P.O. Box 77845, San Fran-
cisco, CA 94197)

Exploring Colorado Wilderness Areas by Scott S. Warren
(The Mountaineers, 1011 S.W. Klickitat Way, Seattle,
WA 98134)

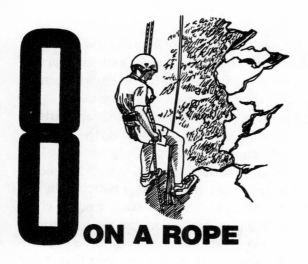

8
ON A ROPE

Although people tend to say, "I climbed three fourteeners this summer," what they usually mean is, "I hiked up three fourteeners this summer." But semantics aside, mountains provide a continuum from hiking to scrambling and finally to climbing in the real sense of the word. A hiker might scramble up some steep, rocky sections, using hands as well as feet. A climber uses technical equipment—ropes, various kinds of anchors, and other protective gear—to move on walls of rock.

Advanced climbers who have the skills but eschew reliance on gear may choose what is called free climbing, or they may prefer bouldering, a combination of scrambling and climbing without technical gear. Winter may come, but some climbers can't stay off the vertical, so they go for ice climbing on frozen waterfalls. Colorado is well-endowed with climbing venues of all kinds, many of them astonishingly accessible to major cities, resort towns, and highways.

Many climbers also start learning or continue refining their skills on indoor artificial climbing walls, and some are so content with the challenging but controlled environment of sport climbing that they don't rock climb at all.

Climbing is an activity that demands confident partnering in a vertical world. One climber moves up the rock; the other provides protection via the rope. Only when the lead climber is secure does the second climber begin to move. They lead and follow in a rhythm that is matched in few sports. Rock climbing has also been compared to chess because of the need for concentration and the importance of small, critical moves. The satisfaction and the self-confidence gained from rock climbing is so deep that it has become a popular component of team-building and self-esteem workshops.

Serious and committed climbers are constantly expanding their abilities in terms of the difficulty of their climbs or their attempts to be the first to ascend a previously unclimbed route. But for the new climber, every route is an accomplishment and a first ascent. Technical climbing is clearly not a do-it-yourself sport. Most of the "climbing accidents" reported in the media involve inexperienced, ill-equipped amateurs scrambling around on rocks where they have no business being. Climbing instruction is readily available throughout the Colorado Rockies, so there's no excuse for anyone to be monkeying around on rock without it.

CLIMBING TERMS

Climbing terms are broad and have changed as rock-climbing technique has evolved. Here are some common terms and their generally understood, broad definitions:

Belay: To protect the lead climber by controlling the rope attached to his or her harness

Carabiner: A common piece of climbing hardware (a spring-loaded loop that clicks onto other protective devices attached to the rock)

Crack climbing: Climbing any crack, including jamming and other techniques

Crampons: A device with metal prongs that attaches to the boot sole to provide traction on snow and ice

Edging: Climbing on small footholds

Face climbing: Climbing on the face of the rock without using cracks; includes using toe- and fingerholds

Free climbing: Placing but not directly using protection to move up the rock

Friction climbing: Climbing steep, relatively smooth rock with no holds or few minimal holds; technique relies on friction of feet to keep from slipping while moving up the rock

Harness: A seat-like web belt to which the climber attaches the rope

Jamming: Jamming hands and feet into a vertical or near-vertical crack in order to move up the rock

Lead: As a verb, to be the first climber on a pitch; as a noun, the distance between belay points

Nuts: Tapered pieces of metal of various sizes, with slings or wires attached, that are wedged into cracks to guide the rope as climbers move up the rock

Pitch: One section of route, commonly the length of the rope

Rack: A set of equipment for technical climbing, including belay or rappel device, carabiners, nuts, and other gear

Rappel: A controlled slide down a rope

Roof: A rock overhang

163

Top roping: Belaying a climber from a rope anchored above
Traverse: To move laterally or diagonally across a rock face

CLASSES OF ROUTES

Most American climbing guidebooks and climbers use the Yosemite Decimal System in describing mountain routes. There are two parts to the system. The first is a Roman numeral indicating a mountain route's overall "grade":
Grade I—A short day climb of up to 3,000 vertical feet and/or three pitches of technical climbing
Grade II—A day climb of up to 6,000 vertical feet and/or six pitches of technical climbing
Grade III—A very long day climb of up to 10,000 vertical feet and/or ten pitches of technical climbing and/or a great deal of Class 3 scrambling
Grade IV—A very long day climb of more than 10,000 vertical feet and/or ten pitches of technical climbing

The second part of the Yosemite system is an Arabic number that denotes the degree of difficulty of a route's most difficult pitch in dry conditions. This is called a route's "class." Classes 1 to 4, which for most people range from modest hikes to scrambles, are given as simple numbers; Class 5 routes are usually technical climbs, stated as decimals. While pitches up to 5.14 have been accomplished elsewhere, climbers generally find 5.0 to 5.8 on mountains, and 5.10 is generally the most difficult level found in canyons that are popular with Colorado climbers. Pitches can be quite short yet immensely challenging.
Class 1—Hiking trails

Class 2—Hiking and bushwhacking; may involve scree slopes or sections where scrambling is necessary
Class 3—Scrambling
Class 4—Easy technical climbing where a rope and occasional belay are used
Class 5—Technical climbing in ascending order of difficulty from 5.0, requiring ropes, slings, nuts, and other protection

Climbers tackling routes on major mountains need to be aware of the steepness of a route's most difficult snow or ice sections, if there are any, and how much exposure it has, while technical climbers need to know the ratings of both the most difficult free-climbing and technical-climbing sections of any route.

WHERE TO CLIMB

Aspen Area

Aspen is synonymous with skiing in winter and cultural activities (Aspen Music Festival, DanceAspen, and others) and hiking in summer, but it is also a traditional and important climbing center. The granite cliffs off the Independence Pass road—notably the three Grotto Cliffs, Nude Buttress, and Weller Slab—continue to lure climbers, as do selected areas of the Elk Range. The fabled Maroon Bells, however, which are constantly photographed and frequently hiked, are less often climbed because much of the rock is crumbly. The USFS Aspen District office has current information.

Aspen Resort Association
425 Rio Grande Place
Aspen, CO 81611
800-262-7736, 970-925-1940

Black Canyon of the Gunnison

The Gunnison River has carved cliffs up to 2,700 feet deep—or high if you are climbing—that have a reputation as some of Colorado's largest, most challenging, and nastiest rock walls. The most frequently climbed area is North Chasm View Wall, specifically the south face.

Because it is a chasm, climbers must haul equipment down before they can climb up. This area, administered by the National Park Service, is not for new or dilettante climbers. The ranger station on the North Rim generally has the most detailed information for climbers.

Black Canyon of the Gunnison National Monument
P.O. Box 1648
Montrose, CO 81401
970-249-7036

Boulder Area

Boulder's quasi-official symbol is the Flatirons, a trio of up-tilted rocks south and west of the city and accessible from a popular city park. Among Colorado's most classic and most popular climbs, these sandstone formations are called the First, Second, and Third Flatirons. The spires a few miles to the south are known as the Maiden and the Matron and are more challenging. The lower narrows of Boulder Canyon provide a number of excellent granite walls and formations, and most are easily accessible, being just steps from the road westward from Boulder toward Nederland. From the Dome, just a mile from the canyon mouth, to Castle Rock, another ten miles up the road, crack climbing, face climbing, and some winter ice-climbing venues abound. But perhaps the most famous of all the Boulder climbing areas is Eldorado Canyon, known for solid, steep sandstone pitches aand for providing world-class face-climbing options. Located south of the city, Eldorado Canyon State Park is a fee area, and park administrators also close Eldorado routes during the peregrine-falcon nesting season. The area's best bouldering is on Flagstaff Mountain, with some also available at Red Rocks Park, just north of the mouth of Boulder Canyon.

Boulder Convention and Visitors Bureau
2440 Pearl Street
Boulder, CO 80301
303-442-2911

Colorado Springs Area

To sightseers, the Garden of the Gods' towers, turrets, buttresses, and fanciful figures carved by nature are objects of wonder. To rock climbers, the best of the sandstone formations in this scenic city park are goals. Montezuma Tower and North and South Gateway Towers are among the most popular. As a result of the pressure of ardent climbers, a stringent permit system is now in place, and climbers must register at the park visitors center. Anyone climbing more than ten feet above the ground must have proper technical equipment.

Turkey Rocks, between Woodland Park and Deckers northwest of Colorado Springs, are known for some of Colorado's best crag climbing, as well as for interesting face routes. Two nearby walls, Turkey Rock and Turkey Trails, each about 250 feet in height, provide the most notable climbing. Cynical Pinnacle, believed by many to be even better, is closed during the long peregrine-falcon nesting season.

Colorado Springs Convention and Visitors Bureau and
    South Central Colorado Tourism Region
Both at:
104 South Cascade Avenue, Suite 104
Colorado Springs, CO 80903
719-635-7506

Rocky Mountain National Park

Lumpy Ridge and Twin Owls in the park's northeastern corner draw climbers to their granite faces and shallow cracks, but strong, hard-core climbers often opt instead for the big walls of Hallet's Peak, Cathedral Spires, and especially Longs Peak's spectacular East Face. Many hikers do some scrambling and handwork even on the Keyhole route, Longs's easiest ascent, which wraps nearly around the mountain, but most of the scores of other options are out-and-out technical. Well before these mountains attained National Park status, Longs Peak was already such a popular climbing spot that a sturdy cable was anchored into the rock in a north-facing couloir just below the summit.

In 1973, rangers removed the cable but left some of the bolts, providing today's climbers with convenient anchors for their ropes. The Cable Route is tough enough for most, especially given the altitude, but it pales compared with the East Face. The easiest way up this sheer wall is a classic mountaineering route called Kieners, while the 1,000-foot slab known as the Diamond is one of the toughest. Several glaciers and numerous deep chasms into which snow packs distinguish the high peaks of Rocky Mountain National Park and also offer fine snow climbs.

Rocky Mountain National Park
Estes Park, CO 80517
303-586-2371

Telluride Area

Located in the magnificent San Juan Range, historic Telluride nestles at the end of a box canyon with rock-walled mountains all around. Some of the best climbing areas are a dozen or so miles south of town, near the settlements of Ophir and Ames. The deeply fractured granite of Ophir Wall, Ames Wall, and Cracked Canyon are among the West's premier climbing areas. The region also offers exceptional ice climbing on Bridalveil Falls, above Telluride, and fine bouldering opportunities on the Idorada Boulders. Lizardhead Peak was reputedly one of the first technical rock climbs in the United States.

Telluride Chamber Resort Association
P.O. Box 653
Telluride, CO 81435
303-728-3041

MOUNTAINEERING

Those who are into hiking, backpacking, and climbing but want to expand their competition in all-around backcountry skills, can sign up for a mountaineering course, available from most climbing schools. Such a course would generally cover low-impact camping, rock climbing, snow climbing, map and compass skills, and often natural history and environmental considerations as well.

CLIMBING INSTRUCTION AND GUIDE SERVICES

Most of these guide services offer regular or on-demand classes in all levels of rock climbing. Guided climbs, multi-day rock-climbing camps, and instruction in general mountaineering or specific snow- or ice-climbing skills can often be arranged as well. In addition to schools and guide services, you can hire a certified guide to teach or lead a climb. A list of members is available from:
Adventures to the Edge
P.O. Box 91
707 Elk Avenue
Crested Butte, CO970-349-5219

American Climbing Guides Association
P.O. Box 2128
Estes Park, CO 80517
970-586-0571

Climbing Schools
American Wilderness Experience
P.O. Box 1486

Boulder, CO 80306
303-444-3999

Aspen Alpine Guides
P.O. Box 659
Aspen, CO 81612
970-925-6618

Backcountry Experience
780 Main Avenue
Durango, CO 81302
800-642-5389, 970-259-0370

The Boulder Rock School
2952 Baseline Road
Boulder, CO 80303
800-836-4008, 303-447-2804

Colorado Mountain School
P.O. Box 2062
Estes Park, CO 80157
970-586-5758

Elk Mountain Guides
P.O. Box 10327
Aspen, CO 81612
970-927-9377

Front Range Mountain Guides
P.O. Box 17294
Boulder, CO 80308
303-666-5523

Great Horizons Rock Climbing School
504 Maxwell Avenue
Boulder, CO 80304
303-628-4646

High Peaks Mountain Guides
P.O. Box 1519
1 West First Street
Nederland, CO 80466
303-258-7436

International Alpine School
P.O. Box 3037
Eldorado Springs, CO 80025
303-494-4974 (Boulder), 970-626-5722 (Ridgway)

Ouray Victorian Inn
50 Third Avenue
Ouray, CO 81427
800-443-7362

Paragon Guides
P.O. Box 130
Vail, CO 81658
970-926-5299

Rocky Mountain Climbing School
P.O. Box 2432
Aspen, CO 81612
970-925-7625

Rocky Mountain Ventures
P.O. Box 775046

Steamboat Springs, CO 80477
970-879-4857

SouthWest Adventures
P.O. Box 3242
780 Main Avenue
Durango, CO 81302
800-642-5389, 970-259-0370

Sundance Adventure Center
3371 Gold Lake Road
Ward, CO 80481
303-459-0225

TIPS FOR CLIMBERS

In general, climbing is risky and not for the unpracticed. The stakes are high, which is what provides the adrenaline rush, but playing around on rock with inadequate equipment and/or training is simply foolish.

While some of Colorado's canyon walls and rock faces are solid and ideal for technical climbing, others are what climbers call "rotten" and cannot be relied on to hold a person's weight. A guide—human or book—is invaluable in determining where to climb safely. Climbers must also be aware of seasonal closures, normally in raptor habitats.

What to Take

Take the usual water, sunscreen, and other Colorado outdoor staples, plus climbing wear or other comfortable pants

173

and tops that allow freedom of motion. In addition, you'll need a helmet, rock shoes, harness, rope, chalk and bag, and a rack of hardware suitable for the anticipated climb. These are normally supplied by climbing schools or available from climbing and mountaineering shops. For snow and ice climbing, add suitable protective clothing, ice ax, plastic boots, and crampons.

MOUNTAINEERING AND OTHER WILDERNESS SKILLS

It is difficult to know where in a book such as this to place Outward Bound, which is as much about the philosophy of self-reliance and team reliance in the wilderness as it is about building skills in a variety of environments. But this chapter is as suitable as any, because the rope skills that are part of so many Outward Bound courses are the ones most people associate with this organization.

A typical domestic Outward Bound course is anywhere from five to eighteen days, with a format consisting of a "training phase," a team expedition, a solo, a team-building service project, a final group expedition, and a personal test of new endurance and fitness as the "concluding phase." Courses focus on alpine mountaineering, rock climbing, winter mountaineering, desert and canyon exploration, whitewater river exploration, and "multi-environment exploration."

There are regular programs for adults, college students, teens, executives, and women. Particular curriculum modifications adapt the Outward Bound approach to people recovering from substance abuse, couples seeking to improve support and communication skills, cancer patients and survivors, and other special needs. Course sites are in various Colorado mountain ranges and rivers, as well as in other states and abroad.

Colorado Outward Bound School
945 Pennsylvania Street
Denver, CO 80203
800-477-2627, 303-837-0880

The kinds of ideas embodied in Outward Bound's approach also have been adapted by other organizations that believe that the "controlled adventure" outdoors is key to team building, problem solving, conflict mediation, and other experiences that help individuals and groups make the most of their potential. One of the largest such centers in Colorado is:
Snow Mountain Ranch—YMCA of the Rockies
P.O. Box 169
Winter Park, CO 80482
970-887-2152, 303-443-4743 (metro Denver)

HOW YOU CAN HELP

With about 500,000 Americans participating in rock and ice climbing, and more getting interested every year, the environmental impact on places that previously saw few people is growing. Local climbing clubs and shops occasionally organize chalk cleanup projects in nearby climbing areas. In addition, the Access Fund, which is Colorado-based but national in scope, works to protect the natural resources used by climbers while preserving access to rock and ice. The fund purchases land and represents the climbing community in negotiations with public-land managers.

The Access Fund
P.O. Box 17010
Boulder, CO 80308

READING LIST

Colorado Front Range Bouldering by Bob Horan (Chockstone Press, P.O. Box 3505, Evergreen, CO 80439)
Colorado Front Range Crags by Peter Hubbel (Chockstone Press)
Rocky Mountain National Park, *Flatiron Classics*, and *Colorado's Indian Peaks* all by Gerry Roach (Fulcrum Publishing, 350 Indiana Street, Golden, CO 80401)
Rocky Mountain Rock Climbs by John Harlin III (Chockstone Press)

9 DOWN A MOUNTAIN

The collective marketing organization for Colorado's two dozen-odd ski areas is called Colorado Ski Country USA. This was an ambitious and optimistic name when the organization was founded, but today is not far from the truth. In-state and visiting skiers annually chalk up close to twelve million visits to the state's lift-served ski areas. They range from low-key, local ski areas where prices are moderate and the atmosphere relaxed, to glamorous, world-class resorts where the prices may rise to the stratosphere but the facilities and programs put them among the top ski meccas on earth.

What attracts skiers of all tastes and with all sorts of budgets is a combination of snow conditions and accessibility. The typical winter storms that douse the Rockies with cloud-light powder start over the Pacific, lose moisture as they pass over the deserts of Arizona or Nevada, and fall as skiable fluff on Colorado's high mountains. To ensure an early start to the season and an adequate skiable surface throughout the winter, many areas also have installed extensive snowmaking systems, and snow grooming had been refined to a high art as well.

All ski areas, large and small, offer ski terrain for all ability levels, food service, rental equipment, skiing and snowboarding instruction for adults and children, day care for youngsters too young to ski, and ski patrols for rescue and first aid. Beyond that, everything is merely a matter of scale. A modest mountain will have older, slower lifts (mostly double and perhaps triple chairlifts, none of them high-speed) serving a moderate amount of acreage. A major ski area also will have high-speed four-place chairlifts (and perhaps a gondola or two where skiers ride uphill in enclosed cabins) serving more expansive terrain.

Technically, Colorado's ski season kicks off in October or early November, with Keystone and Loveland usually opening within hours of each other. It winds down in June or July when Arapahoe Basin shuts down, but most people consider ski season to be from Thanksgiving to Easter. Prices for lift tickets, lodging, and often other components of a ski trip vary greatly through the season. The best prices are before Christmas and at the very end of the season. January and sometimes late March offer excellent values, while the Christmas–New Year holiday and February command the highest prices and the biggest crowds.

In addition to lift-served skiing, downhillers have a choice of taking snowcats or helicopters to ski pristine snowfields, sometimes adjacent to a ski area, sometimes not. Skiers and snowboarders who don't want the season to end traditionally hike up popular long-lasting snowfields and ski down again, in spring and well into summer.

TYPES OF TERRAIN

The trail designation system used in the United States marks a mountain's easiest runs with a green circle, the more difficult ones with a blue square, and the most difficult ones with a black triangle. Skiers sometimes misinterpret these signs as symbols for beginner, intermediate, and expert terrain, but in truth, they indicate the relative difficulty among trails on one specific mountain and are not absolutes. Therefore, a black-diamond trail at Silver-Creek might be an easy blue on Aspen Mountain. Some areas also have hybrid trail markers to further differentiate them, such as a green circle within a blue square (suitable for "advanced novice" skiers), a pair of blue squares (high midlevel terrain), or double diamonds (super-steep, for experts only).

Most green-circle and many blue-square slopes and trails are groomed nightly by fleets of snowcats. Black-diamond terrain, which is rarely or never groomed, might be steep chutes, steep mogul runs (a mogul is a hump of snow built up when many skiers turn in the same place), glades (trees spaced widely enough to ski between), or treeless bowls.

WHERE TO SKI

Although you ski mountains and not statistics, numbers mean more in the skiing game than in most other non-scored, individual sports. The important figures designate base and summit elevations (measured in feet above sea level), vertical drop (the difference in altitude between

179

these two elevations), skiable acreage (generally cleared runs, with tree skiing thrown in as a nonmeasured bonus), number of runs (count of open slopes and cut trails), number of lifts (gondolas, high-speed express chairlifts, conventional-speed chairlifts of various configurations, and surface lifts), hourly lift capacity (skiers per hour if every seat on every lift is filled, which, taken in the context of skiable acreage and vertical drop, gives a good idea of how crowded an area is at maximum), average annual snowfall (in inches), and snowmaking coverage (given as a percentage of the skiable acreage or as a fixed number of acres). These statistics can change as ski areas add new lifts, upgrade existing ones, enhance snowmaking, or expand terrain. These numbers do not reflect the quality of the skiing, specific snow conditions, the majesty of the scenery, the presence or absence of lift lines (lots of fast lifts handle more skiers than a few slow ones), or the congeniality of one's companions, but they are useful for comparing areas.

The ski areas within two hours of metro Denver-Boulder (A-Basin, Breckenridge, Copper Mountain, Eldora, Keystone, Loveland, Vail, and Winter Park) tend to get pressured on weekends by hordes of Front Range aficionados. Especially after a good snowstorm, the traffic on I-70 can reach epic rush-hour proportions. By contrast, more distant destination resorts are relatively uncrowded on Saturdays and Sundays. In addition to gateway airports in Denver and Colorado Springs, regional airports (some with direct ski-season jet service from distant cities such as Chicago, Dallas/Fort Worth, Chicago, Los Angeles, and Minneapolis) are at Durango, Eagle, Grand Junction, Gunnison, Hayden, and Montrose, and local airports are in Aspen, Steamboat Springs, and Telluride.

General information on Colorado skiing and ski resorts is available from:
Colorado Ski Country USA
1560 Broadway, Suite 1440
Denver, CO 80202
303-837-0783

CSCUSA's recorded statewide snow-conditions reports are available from 800-825-SNOW; free computerized conditions reports are available from TravelBank Systems via modem from 303-671-7669.

Arapahoe Basin

America's highest lift-served mountain is known for challenging skiing—much of it above the timberline. A-Basin is a winter-powder haven and a spring-skiing mecca. The views and the rarefied air are among the state's most pristine. There are plans to install snowmaking and extend the season through the summer, which would make this the only lift-served summer-skiing area in the Rockies. The nearest lodging is six miles away at Keystone, whose parent company also owns Breckenridge and offers a fully interchangeable, three-mountain lift ticket. Copper Mountain is included in the Ski the Summit pass.
Base: 10,800 feet
Summit: 12,050 feet
Vertical: 2,250 feet
Acreage: 490
Trails: 61
Lifts: 5
Lift capacity: 6,066

Snowfall: 360 inches
Snowmaking: none
Keystone Resort
P.O. Box 38
Keystone, CO 80435
Snow conditions: 970-468-4111
Lodging reservations: 800-222-0188

Arrowhead Mountain

This boutique resort with one high-speed quad chairlift and one beginner lift has been purchased by Vail Associates. With the construction of one new lift, it is scheduled to be linked into the terrain of Beaver Creek for the 1995–96 ski season. The Beaver Creek numbers reflect that projected combination.

Aspen Highlands

Long the odd mountain out in the Aspen skiing scene, Highlands is now operated by the Aspen Skiing Co. and accepts the same lift ticket as Aspen Mountain, Snowmass, and Tiehack. The ski company has embarked on a long-needed upgrade, adding two high-speed quad chairlifts to access a huge vertical. The terrain is tall and skinny, with a confined base area tapering upward to a narrower ridge. The runs are varied, including a galaxy of steep bowls and newly opened glades off the sides of the main mountain.
Base: 8,040 feet
Summit: 11,675 feet
Vertical: 3,635 feet

Acreage: 597
Trails: 77
Lifts: 9
Lift capacity: 9,145
Snowfall: 300 inches
Snowmaking: 110 acres
Aspen Skiing Company
P.O. Box 1248
Aspen, CO 81612
Snow conditions: 970-925-1221
Lodging reservations: 800-525-6200

Aspen Mountain

Looming over Aspen, the gorgeous nineteenth-century silver boomtown reborn as the ultimate glamour resort of the latter twentieth century, Aspen Mountain is best for intermediate and advanced skiers. A six-place gondola links the town and the summit, with most of the skiing concentrated at the top, where the splendor of the scenery matches the challenges of the slopes. This classic mountain is famous for mogul-studded steeps and fantastic tree skiing, but it also offers broad cruising boulevards for intermediate skiers. It is the only one of the four Aspen ski areas where snowboarding is prohibited.
Base: 7,945 feet
Summit: 11,212 feet
Vertical: 3,267 feet
Acreage: 631
Trails: 76
Lifts: 8
Lift capacity: 10,775

Snowfall: 300 inches
Snowmaking: 310 acres
Aspen Skiing Company
P.O. Box 1248
Aspen, CO 81612
Snow report: 970-925-1221
Lodging reservations: 800-525-6200

Beaver Creek

The name Beaver Creek is synonymous with luxurious living, but the skiing is first-rate, varied, and not just for the carriage trade. High-speed lifts climb up two sides of the high valley that shelters the resort development, and ski terrain surrounds it in a huge area topped by several peaks. Though it is best known for wide, congenial cruising runs for novice and intermediate skiers, there are also stunning steeps on Grouse Mountain and a quartet of long, consistently pitched mogul runs collectively called the Birds of Prey. Linkage with Arrowhead, planned for 1995–96*, will increase the ski area's vertical and, for the first time, offer lift access from the Eagle River Valley.
Base: 7,400
Summit: 11,440
Vertical: 4,040
Acreage: 1,400 (approx.)
Trails: 75 (approx.)
Lifts: 13
Lift capacity: 20,000 (approx.)
Snowfall: 330 inches
Snowmaking: 445 acres
Vail Associates

P.O. Box 7
Vail, CO 81658
Snow report: 970-476-4888
Lodging reservations: 800-622-3131
*Statistics reflect consolidated areas and, in some cases, are approximations before the lift-and-trail connection between the two was announced; the original Beaver Creek base is at 8,100 feet and the original Arrowhead summit is at 9,100.

Breckenridge

Three sprawling interconnected mountains, the southern-most peaks of the Tenmile Range, rise from a delightful Victorian town and offer as great a range of terrain as any ski area in Colorado. Peak 8 is largely for novices, Peak 10 is for advanced skiers and experts, and Peak 9 has something for everyone, including a great selection of midlevel runs. Tree-free bowls and snowfields crown the summits, while steep mogul runs and wide white boulevards cascade down the mountainsides to the valleys separating these three peaks. Breck's mogul runs are famous, and it was one of the first major areas to embrace snowboarding. One lift ticket is valid for Breckenridge, A-Basin, and Keystone.
Base: 9,600 feet
Summit: 12,998 feet
Vertical: 3,398 feet
Acreage: 1,915
Trails: 126
Lifts: 16
Lift capacity: 24,430
Snowfall: 255 inches

Colorado Outdoor Activity Guide

Snowmaking: 362 acres
Breckenridge Ski Area
P.O. Box 1058
Breckenridge, CO 80424
Snow report: 970-453-6118
Lodging reservations: 800-800-2732

Copper Mountain

Located right along I-70 just seventy-five miles from Denver, Copper is ultra-accessible, but it's not merely roadside skiing. Copper is highly regarded for its excellent trail layout, which is very neatly segmented by ability level. Copper Peak and Union Peak, and all the trails and bowls laid out on a respectable vertical, provide intermediate and advanced skiers with their own playgrounds, and there is an additional excellent novice area called Union Creek with wide, gentle slopes. This outstanding family resort has a top-notch children's program and a modern, walk-around village at the base. Snowcat skiing access introduced skiers to Copper Bowl on the mountain's back side in 1994–95, with lift access projected for the following winter.
Base: 9,712 feet
Summit: 12,313 feet
Vertical: 2,601 feet
Acreage: 1,360 feet
Trails: 98
Lifts: 19
Lift capacity: 28,250
Snowfall: 255 inches
Snowmaking: 270 acres
Copper Mountain

186

P.O. Box 3001
Copper Mountain, CO 80443
Snow report: 970-968-2100
Lodging reservations: 800-458-8386

Crested Butte

It's a toss-up as to whether skiers are more enchanted by the quaint mountain town of Crested Butte or the namesake ski resort of Crested Butte Mountain. The skiing has two main strengths. It is a wonderful learn-to-ski area with excellent novice runs and one of Colorado's premier venues for ungroomed super-steep terrain for experts. The intermediate trails are really good too, but they are eclipsed by the two extremes on the spectrum. Most of the easiest terrain can be reached directly from the slopeside village of Mt. Crested Butte (another namesake), while the most challenging is approached by a T-bar or platterpull—and perhaps a hike, if untracked powder is the goal. It's a rad mountain for cliff-jumping, stump-hopping extreme skiers and for telemarkers, who launched their sport on the Butte's slopes. Since 1991, the resort has offered free skiing and free beginner instruction—no strings attached—for several weeks between Thanksgiving and Christmas.
Base: 9,100 feet
Summit: 11,875 feet
Vertical: 2,775 feet
Acreage: 1,162 feet
Trails: 85
Lifts: 13
Lift capacity: 15,960
Snowfall: 260 inches

Snowmaking: 242 acres
Crested Butte Mountain Resort
P.O. Box A
Mt. Crested Butte, CO 81225
Snow report: 970-349-2323
Lodging reservations: 800-544-8448

Cuchara Valley

Cuchara, Colorado's southernmost area, is also the state's renaissance resort. After being shut completely for several years, the ski area reopened in 1992–93. It is a congenial, low-key mountain where the climate is mild and prices are moderate. The main chairlift is a base-to-summit lift accessing most of the mountain with its variety of mostly intermediate runs. Cuchara's sheltered beginner area is at the base. A fine little bowl that's a short hike from the highest lift provides advanced skiers with their own ungroomed turf. Cuchara offers variety, though not on a grand scale.
Base: 9,248 feet
Summit: 10, 810 feet
Vertical: 1,562 feet
Acreage: 230
Trails: 24
Lifts: 4
Lift capacity: 5,600
Snowfall: 200 inches
Snowmaking: 170 acres
Cuchara Valley Resort
946 Panadero Avenue
Cuchara, CO 81055

Snow report: 719-742-3163
Lodging reservations: 800-227-4436

Eldora

This midsized mountain offers day and night skiing with
easy access from Denver and Boulder. (There's even a bus
that's part of the metro-area transit system, the only
Colorado ski area served by inexpensive public transporta-
tion.) The front side of the main mountain is an amalgam of
intermediate and advanced runs, while Corona Bowl on
the back side is geared for advanced and expert skiers. The
beginner slope is off to the side, out of the major traffic
lanes. Its snowmaking might is increasingly annually, and
its snowboarding and racing programs are the peer of
larger areas.
Base: 9,200 feet
Summit: 10,600 feet
Vertical: 1,400 feet
Acreage: 386
Trails: 43
Lifts: 9
Lift capacity: 7,500
Snowfall: 185 inches
Snowmaking: 190 acres
Eldora Mountain Resort
P.O. Box 1697
Nederland, CO 80466
Snow report: 303-440-8700
Lodging reservations: 303-440-8700

Howelson Ski Area

Located right in the town of Steamboat Springs, Howelson is a truly historic ski area. (Ski jumping started there in 1914.) This small, steep hill and the Little League–style ski-training programs that use it turn local youngsters into ski champions: jumpers, Alpine skiers, and freestyle skiers. For visitors, its main appeals are night skiing and one of two recreational bobsled runs in Colorado. (The other is at mighty Vail.)

Base: 6,696 feet
Summit: 7,136 feet
Vertical: 440 feet
Acreage: 70
Trails: 15
Lifts: 3
Lift capacity: 2,058
Snowfall: 250 inches
Snowmaking: 35 acres
Howelson Ski Area
P.O. Box 775088
Steamboat Springs, CO 80477
Snow report: 303-879-8499
Lodging reservations: 800-922-2722

Keystone

Keystone is many things to many skiers. The ski area's three interconnected mountains, strung one behind the other like charms on a bracelet, have different personalities and appeal to different levels of skiers. The original Keystone Mountain is a haven for novice and intermediate skiers—and Colorado's night-skiing capital as well. North Peak is a mogul-studded mountain for iron-legged experts. The Outback offers big bumps and great glades, while the hike-to Outback Bowls have terrific tree skiing. Keystone is the only area in North America with two six-place gondolas (one up Keystone Mountain and the other across to North Peak). Snowboarding is not permitted at Keystone, but the area is skiable on a joint lift ticket with Arapahoe Basin and Breckenridge. Keystone's resort development consists of a lakeside village center with additional condominiums and homes tucked into the woods.

Base: 9,300 feet
Summit: 12,200 feet
Vertical: 2,900 feet
Acreage: 1,737
Trails: 89
Lifts: 19
Lift capacity: 26,582
Snowfall: 230 inches
Snowmaking: 849 acres
Keystone Resort
P.O. Box 38
Keystone, CO 80435
Snow report: 970-468-4111
Lodging reservations: 800-222-0188

Loveland Ski Area

Located just sixty miles and half a mountain pass from Denver, Loveland offers Colorado's best ratio of skiable terrain close to the state's major population center and transportation hub. The high-altitude area has two components:

the gentle beginner sector called Loveland Valley and the high-Alpine cirque called Loveland Basin, which records the second greatest annual snowfall of any Colorado ski area and a long season that usually starts in October and runs through mid-May. The Basin is largely above the timberline, offering grand powder and gorgeous views. The nearest lodging is in the old mining towns of Georgetown and Idaho Springs, east of Loveland.

Base: 10,600 feet

Summit: 12,280 feet

Vertical: 1,680 feet

Acreage: 836

Trails: 60

Lifts: 5

Lift capacity: 12,258

Snowfall: 375 inches

Snowmaking: 159 acres

Loveland Ski Area

P.O. Box 899

Georgetown, CO 80444

Snow report: 800-736-3SKI, 970-569-3203

Lodging reservations: 800-225-LOVE

Monarch

This low-key, moderately priced ski area—one of Colorado's oldest—on the east side of Monarch Pass is a central Colorado favorite and one of the state's powder havens. Terrain from mild to wild, plus a snowcat operation into a couple of adjacent valleys, mean there's skiing and snowboarding terrain for everyone from tiny tots to powderhounds. Just a handful of lifts give access to surprisingly expansive terrain for a mountain with such modest statistics. There's everything from wide slopes and cut trails to ample tree skiing and treeless snowfields. The nearest accommodations are a couple of miles away, with more down in the Arkansas River Valley towns of Poncha Springs and Salida.

Base: 10,790 feet
Summit: 11,950 feet
Vertical: 1,160 feet
Acreage: 637
Trails: 60
Lifts: 4
Lift capacity: 4,600
Snowfall: 350 inches
Snowmaking: none
Monarch Ski Resort
1 Powder Place
Monarch, CO 81227
Snow report: 800-332-3668
Lodging reservations: 800-332-3668

Powderhorn

Located on the side of Grand Mesa, this is western Colorado's home hill. Lifts angle off in two directions from the main base area. Powderhorn's twenty miles of modest trails are largely for intermediate skiers, but the views toward the Book Cliffs from nearly any part of the trail system are four-star by any standards. A platterpull serves a good beginner hill right near the base lodge. Though it's known more as a congenial day-skiing area and low-key resort rather than for tree skiing, Powderhorn altitude

193

means that it also offers some lovely aspen groves, which are excellent when there's fresh powder.
Base: 8,200 feet
Summit: 9,800 feet
Vertical: 1,600
Acreage: 300
Trails: 54
Lifts: 4
Lift capacity: 4,370
Snowfall: 200 inches
Snowmaking: 50 acres
Powderhorn Ski Corporation
P.O. Box 330
4828 Powderhorn Road
Mesa, CO 81643
Snow report: 970-268-5700
Lodging reservations: 800-241-6997

Purgatory

Colorado's most southwestern ski resort is a sun-kissed ridge with skiing that becomes progressively harder as you move away from the base village at the eastern end of the trail system. A small novice area below the village is perfect for learning the rudiments of skiing, and the easiest terrain is right near the base. Intermediate trails predominate halfway back, while the most challenging runs, particularly the group of mogul trails collectively known as the Legends, are the farthest back. While ski-area policies do change, sometimes annually, it is noteworthy that at this writing, children ski free at Purgatory at all times, which makes it heaven for budget-conscious families.

194

Base: 8,793 feet
Summit: 10,822 feet
Vertical: 2,029 feet
Acreage: 722
Trails: 74
Lifts: 9
Lift capacity: 12,700
Snowfall: 250 inches
Snowmaking: 150 acres
Purgatory Ski Resort
1 Skier Place
Durango, CO 81301
Snow report: 800-525-0892
Lodging reservations: 800-525-0892

SilverCreek

This vest-pocket area is one of Colorado's learn-to-ski capitals. A small development nestles at the base of a very easy, very small ski hill and a somewhat harder, somewhat higher one. A slew of innovative programs and facilities geared to thrifty families and beginners make this an ideal place to begin skiing.
Base: 8,202 feet
Summit: 9,202 feet
Vertical: 1,000 feet
Acreage: 248
Trails: 26
Lifts: 4
Lift capacity: 5,400
Snowfall: 180 inches
Snowmaking: 95 acres

SilverCreek
P.O. Box 1110
SilverCreek, CO 80446
Snow report: 800-754-7458
Lodging reservations: 800-754-7458

Ski Cooper

This snow-sure ski area high on Tennessee Pass traces its roots back to the Tenth Mountain Division, America's fabled World War II mountaineering and ski troops. The legend has mellowed into a casual ski area that appeals to those who prefer low prices and no frills to high prices and every frill skiing has come up with. The double-sided mountain has mostly easy runs on the front side and intermediate terrain on the back. Cooper also runs snowcat skiing excursions to nearby Chicago Ridge to appeal to expert skiers and powder fanatics. The nearest accommodations are in Leadville.
Base: 10,500 feet
Summit: 11,700 feet
Vertical: 1,200 feet
Acreage: 385
Trails: 26
Lifts: 4
Lift capacity: 2,000
Snowfall: 250 inches
Snowmaking: none
Ski Cooper
P.O. Box 896
Leadville, CO 80461

Snow report: 719-486-2277
Lodging reservations: 800-748-2057

Ski Sunlight

Sunlight is Colorado's "average" mountain. It's reasonably close to the state's skiing heart. It's midsized, and it's mid-priced as well. The ski terrain arcs around the base area in a long semicircle. More than half of its runs are marked with blue squares, but a fine beginner slope at the base and a relatively new sector of short, super-steep bump runs provide balance on either end. The views toward Mt. Sopris from the uppermost lift are worth the price of a lift ticket at this congenial ski area. There is a small bed base at the resort, but most of the accommodations are in Glenwood Springs.
Base: 7,885 feet
Summit: 9,895 feet
Vertical: 2,010 feet
Acreage: 440
Trails: 50
Lifts: 4
Lift capacity: 5,600
Snowfall: 200 inches
Snowmaking: 10 acres
Ski Sunlight
10901 County Road 117
Glenwood Springs, CO 81601
Snow report: 970-945-7491
Lodging reservations: 800-445-7931

Snowmass

This huge mountain is one of the giants of Colorado skiing. It is the most expansive of the four Aspen areas skiable on one lift ticket and the one that continues to have growth potential. Snowmass's reputation is as an intermediate mountain, and indeed it offers some of the finest cruising terrain in all the land. But it is also an outstanding family area (there's a slopeside resort development that is hard to beat for ski-in, ski-out convenience) and an unheralded spot for experts. (Try Hanging Valley and Elk Camp if you're geared for challenge.) In addition to tackling the area's respectable vertical, those with strong legs and lungs to match can hike an additional 400 vertical feet to ski the Cirque, one of Colorado's steep powder stashes.

Base: 8,223 feet
Summit: 11,835 feet
Vertical: 3,220
Acreage: 2,500
Trails: 72
Lifts: 15
Lift capacity: 21,679
Snowfall: 300 inches
Snowmaking: 62 acres
Aspen Skiing Company
P.O. Box 1248
Aspen, CO 81658
Snow report: 970-925-1221
Lodging reservations: 800-525-6000

Steamboat

Steamboat is the mountain and Steamboat Springs is the nearest town, and between them they comprise a distinctive ski destination. The ski area is huge, sprawling across three interconnected peaks that rise above a plateau that can be reached by the state's first eight-place gondola. From there, lifts fan out in all directions, opening miles of cruising runs, excellent mogul terrain, and some of the best tree skiing in the West. It is also Colorado's northernmost ski resort. Steamboat coined the phrase "champagne powder," and the resort invented the concept of kids ski, stay, and rent equipment free when accompanying parents. The town is a tamed-down Western community known for a friendly, ski-oriented atmosphere.

Base: 6,900 feet
Summit: 10,585 feet
Vertical: 3,685 feet
Acreage: 2,500
Trails: 107
Lifts: 21
Lift capacity: 30,081
Snowfall: 300 inches
Snowmaking: 390 acres
Steamboat Ski & Resort Corporation
2305 Mt. Werner Circle
Steamboat Springs, CO 80487
Snow report: 970-879-7300
Lodging reservations: 800-922-2722

Telluride

This jewel of southwestern Colorado has a reputation for super-steep skiing—heavy on the moguls—amid the unsurpassed scenic splendor of the San Juan Mountains. The expert runs are justifiably famous (including the newest parcel, a hike-up area called Gold Hill, which adds more than 350 feet to the vertical), but it also offers excellent beginner terrain and fine midlevel runs. Long runs are a hallmark of Telluride skiing, and excellent snow and an absence of crowds further enhance the experience. On one side of the ski area is the picturesque Victorian town of Telluride, while the newer Telluride Mountain Village nestles in the cusp of the expansive trail network.

Base: 8,723 feet
Summit: 11,890 feet
Vertical: 3,165 feet
Acreage: 1,050
Trails: 64
Lifts: 10
Lift capacity: 10,000
Snowfall: 300 inches
Snowmaking: 155 acres
Telluride Ski & Golf Company
P.O. Box 11155
Telluride, CO 81435
Snow report: 970-728-3614
Lodging reservations: 800-525-3455

Tiehack

This twin-peaked ski area (which previously has been called Buttermilk, Buttermilk/Tiehack, and Buttermilk Mountain) would be a commendable destination else-where, but at Aspen, where the scale is large and standards are high, it is the resort town's beginner area. It's true that entry-level skiing and snowboarding lessons are concen-trated here, but there are also long, winsome intermediate runs, steep racing trails, and fine powder-holding glades that don't generally receive the regard they merit. With the addition of a high-speed chairlift on Main Buttermilk in 1993–94, this member of the Aspen quartet is finally getting more recognition as skiers at least sample it using the lift ticket that's good at Tiehack as well as at Aspen Mountain, Aspen Highlands, and Snowmass.

Base: 7,870 feet
Summit: 9,900 feet
Vertical: 2,030 feet
Acreage: 410
Trails: 45
Lifts: 7
Lift capacity: 7,500
Snowfall: 200 inches
Snowmaking: 108 acres
Aspen Skiing Company
P.O. Box 1248
Aspen, CO 81658
Snow report: 970-925-1221
Lodging reservations: 800-525-6200

Vail

By most measures, this is the giant not just of Colorado skiing, but of American skiing. Its scale, facilities (including seven high-speed quad chairlifts, the most anywhere), terrain (scores of trails plus seven nearly tree-free back-side bowls), and outstanding ski-school programs for adults and children are unmatched. From the top of the Outer Mongolia platterpull at the eastern extreme of Vail's vast terrain to the Cascade four-place chairlift on the western end,

201

Vail's trails stretch seven miles. Gold Peak, Vail Mountain, Mid-Vail, the Back Bowls, the Far East, and Lions Head are the major ski sectors. Each one merits exploring, as does the sparkling Alpine-style village at the base. Vail, skiable on the same pass with Beaver Creek, is one of the country's upscale resorts, but fans affirm that the quality and quantity of Vail's offerings are worth every penny from the purse and every pass of the credit card.

Base: 8,200 feet
Summit: 11,450 feet
Vertical: 3,250 feet
Acreage: 4,014
Trails: 121
Lifts: 25
Lift capacity: 41,855
Snowfall: 345 inches
Snowmaking: 274 acres
Vail Associates
P.O. Box 7
Vail, CO 81658
Snow report: 970-476-4888
Lodging reservations: 800-525-2257

Winter Park

Winter Park is one of Colorado's classic ski areas, with a history that stretches back more than half a century. The original web of trails has grown to include the steep mogul trails of Mary Jane; the wonderful intermediate trails and beguiling glades of Mary Jane's Backside; the varied and rarely crowded Vasquez Ridge sector; and Parsenn Bowl, a treeless high-mountain sector that was most recently added to the Winter Park family. The area has an outstanding children's program, a fine new beginner area, and the best program for handicapped skiers in the country. Ample accommodations are nearby.

Base: 9,000 feet
Summit: 12,060 feet
Vertical: 3,060 feet
Acreage: 1,358 feet
Trails: 120
Lifts: 20
Lift capacity: 33,700
Snowfall: 345 inches
Snowmaking: 274 acres
Winter Park Resort
P.O. Box 36
Winter Park, CO 80482
Snow report: 970-572-7669
Lodging reservations: 800-729-5813

SNOWBOARDING

This fast-growing sport has been described as transferring the techniques and attitudes of surfing and skateboarding to a snowy environment. Instead of two skis, the rider controls one wide board in a stance that is at a near-right angle to the length of the board. Ski areas that permit it—and that is all but Aspen Mountain and Keystone—now report that between 5 and 20 percent of their lift ticket sales are for snowboarding. Snowboarding instruction is available at all resorts, including introductory lift/lesson/rental equipment packages at many areas.

Because snowboarders use no poles and dislike the

flats, the best runs for snowboarding are those with a consistent pitch and without great transitions or long run-outs. In addition to trails and powder, an increasing number of ski areas have built half-pipes, which are like bobsled runs with twists and banked turns, and special snowboard parks with box jumps, rail slides, log slides, quarter pipes, kickers, bank slides, and other permutations for the riders. Half-pipes are found at A-Basin, Beaver Creek, Breckenridge, Howelson, Loveland, Purgatory, SilverCreek, Snowmass, Steamboat, Sunlight, Tiehack, and Vail. Snowboard parks have been constructed at Breckenridge, Cuchara, Loveland, Monarch, Purgatory, Snowmass, Steamboat, and Sunlight.

SNOWCAT SKIING AND HELI-SKIING

Snowcat skiing and heli-skiing excursions combine the rush of downhill skiing, without the crowds, and the thrill and solitary beauty of the backcountry, without climbing. Most passenger-carrying snowcats, adaptations of the service and grooming vehicles that prowl lift-served ski areas, can haul about a dozen skiers and guides up slopes that would otherwise require hiking. Some cat skiing is right beside an Alpine area; other operations are independent and more isolated. While the photographic image of such experiences is of perfect turns etched in perfect powder, the reality is that safety considerations make it a more deliberate sport involving waiting for the guide to check potential slide hazards and to determine a route. Guides issue avalanche transceivers to participants in case they are wrong and a skier is caught in a slide. While skiers who ply the ever-groomed runs of lift-served ski areas can virtually predict the silkiness of the snow underfoot, skiers of the never-groomed are as likely to confront corn, crud, and chop as seamless powder. A new generation of "fat skis," which resemble waterskis and float above all sorts of unpacked snow, has brought snowcat and heli-skiing within the realm of strong intermediate skiers.

Heli-skiing is very expensive, and cat skiing, while less so, still is costlier than the highest-priced lift ticket. Prices include transportation, use of avalanche transceiver, one or two guides, and lunch and/or snacks. Most operations have half- and full-day options, and some also offer a single-ride sample.

SNOWCAT OPERATORS

Aspen Mountain Powder Tours
P.O. Box 1248
Aspen, CO 81612
800-525-6200, 970-925-1227

Chicago Ridge Snowcat Tours
Ski Cooper
P.O. Box 896
Leadville, CO 80461
719-486-3685

Copper Bowl Snowcats (until lifts are installed)
Copper Mountain
P.O. Box 3001
Copper Mountain, CO 80443
800-458-8386, 970-962-0882

Great Divide Snow Tours
Monarch Ski Resort
1 Powder Place
Monarch, CO 81227
800-332-3668, 719-539-7652

Irwin Lodge
P.O. Box 457
318 Elk Avenue
800-2-IRWIN-2, 970-349-5308

Montezuma Snowcat Tours
Montezuma Road, Box 30-C
Dillon, CO 80435
970-468-0979

Steamboat Powder Cats
P.O. Box 772468
Steamboat Springs, CO 80477
800-288-0543, 970-879-5188

HELI-SKIING OPERATOR

Telluride Heli-Trax
P.O. Box 1560
Telluride, CO 81435
970-728-4904

SKIING FOR THE DISABLED

A visionary Winter Park ski instructor named Hal O'Leary,
who began teaching disabled children and veterans to ski

in 1970, was instrumental in developing adaptive equipment for people with many different types of disabilities, including amputees, paraplegics, and people with multiple sclerosis. His pioneering program has grown into the multisport National Sports Center for the Disabled and inspired other ski areas in Colorado and across the country to provide facilities that enable physically challenged people to share the slopes. Other programs address the needs of blind skiers and those with developmental disabilities. Some programs are free, while others charge a nominal fee for instruction and/or lift tickets. Many operate daily, but advance reservations are always strongly recommended so that appropriately trained instructors are available. Colorado ski areas and their programs for people with disabilities are:

Aspen Handicapped Skiers Program; serves Tiehack,
    Snowmass, Aspen Highlands, Aspen Mountain
BOLD Ski Program (Blind Outdoor Leadership
    Development)
970-925-2086
Handicap lessons
970-923-3293

Breckenridge Outdoor Center
Physical and mental disabilities; serves Arapahoe Basin, Breckenridge, Copper Mountain, and Keystone
970-453-6422

Colorado School for the Blind
Monarch Ski Resort
719-599-5027

Crested Butte Physically Challenged Ski Program
Physical and developmental disabilities; visual and hearing
impairments
970-349-2296

Durango Purgatory Adaptive Sports Association
Physical, developmental, and learning disabilities; hearing
impairment; multiple disabilities
970-259-0374

Eldora Special Recreation Program
Call for details on specifics; available Fridays through Sundays from January to mid-March
303-442-0606

Loveland Disabled Program
Call for details on specifics
800-736-3754

Powderhorn Disabled Center
Call for details on specifics
970-268-5700

Steamboat Disabled Program
Amputees and other physical disabilities; visual and hearing impairment; developmental disabilities
970-879-6111, Ext. 531

Ski Sunlight Disabled Program
Call for details on specifics; also active in Special Olympics
for the developmentally disabled
970-945-7491

Telluride Adaptive Skier Program
Physical and mental disabilities; stroke survivors; visually impaired
970-728-4424

Vail/Beaver Creek Resort Disabled Skiers Program
Physical and learning disabled; visual and hearing impairments; medically challenged children
970-479-2055, 970-479-2085 (T/DD)

Winter Park National Sports Center for the Disabled
Accommodates 40 distinct disabilities with instruction at all levels and adaptive equipment
970-726-5514, Ext. 179

SUMMER SKIING

Through much of the summer, ski-rack-topped cars can be spotted at pullouts along mountain passes and at remote parking lots in odd places. Skiers and snowboarders who just won't quit hike to high snowfields and slide down or ski down from one switchback to another and hitchhike back to their cars. Among the popular summer skiing areas are Berthoud Pass between Empire and Winter Park (there was once a ski area at this location), Independence Pass between Twin Lakes and Aspen (the road is generally plowed out by Memorial Day), Loveland Pass between Loveland Ski Area and Keystone, Imogene Pass near Telluride (a four-wheel-drive road to a high snowfield that's the site of an annual early-July ski race called the Lunar Cup), and St. Mary Glacier (near Idaho Springs and also once a ski area, although the summer skiing is not directly at the old site).

TIPS FOR SKIERS

All the usual cautions found in previous chapters for exercising in high, dry, and cold conditions are applicable for skiing, except that at ski areas, unlike the backcountry, you can always go inside for a hot chocolate, disposable hand-warmers, or even a pair of goggles.

Winter Driving

It is ironic that the big storms that make the Rockies so enticing to ski also make driving to the mountains tricky. While the state's experienced highway crews perform miracles in plowing and sanding highways and controlling avalanches in slide-prone areas, low visibility, slippery road surfaces, and inexperienced drivers can add up to hazards and traffic backups during snowstorms. Colorado does not normally require tire chains on passenger vehicles, but adequate snow tires are required on high passes when conditions are slick (and smart all winter anyway). Four-wheel- and all-wheel-drive vehicles provide an edge in terms of control and safety, but they are no license to speed, tailgate, weave in and out of traffic, or rely on the brakes for quick stops.

Recorded road-conditions reports are available from 303-639-1111 for highways within two hours of Denver (which would include I-70 as far as Vail and U.S. 40 as far as Winter Park and SilverCreek) and 303-639-1234 statewide. Weather reports are available from 303-398-3964.

READING LIST

The Insider's Guide to the Best Skiing in Colorado by Lito Tejada-Flores (Western Eye Press, P.O. Box Telluride, CO 81435)

Rocky Mountain Skiing by Claire Walter (Fulcrum Publishing, 350 Indiana Street, Golden, CO 80104)

Ski Country Access (Access Press, 10 East 53rd Street, New York, NY 10022)

Ski the Rockies by Marc Muench with text by Peter Shelton (Graphic Arts Publishing, P.O. Box 10306, Portland, OR 10306)

Skier's Guide to Colorado by Curtis W. Casewit (Gulf Publishing Company, P.O. Box 2608, Houston, TX 99252)

10

OVER THE SNOW

Cross-country skiing is the consummate winter outdoor activity. The equipment—bindings and boots that allow the foot to flex and the heel to be free from the ski—offer mobility in the tranquil winter world. This ancient form of over-snow travel has been reborn in the last two decades, and its equally venerable kin, snowshoeing, is currently undergoing a boom. Dogsledding is another old form of travel, albeit from different roots, which offers yet another way to move across the snow.

For casual outdoors enthusiasts, cross-country skiing and snowshoeing are low-cost ways to explore the tranquil woods and offer the opportunity to encounter wildlife that is difficult to spot in summer. Both offer a choice of a gentle trek or a grand expedition in the high country, a controlled excursion on groomed trails or a seat-of-the-pants adventure in the backcountry. In addition to providing sheer recreation, skating skis and small snowshoes that fit over running shoes offer incredible winter conditioning.

With copious snowfalls that pack into a forgiving silky surface, Colorado is a state for exceptional cross-country. Dedicated cross-country centers are much like ski areas without lifts. Like Alpine areas, they mark, groom, map, and rate their trails according to difficulty, offering miles of prepared trails. Some are track-set with continuous ski-width grooves etched a comfortable distance apart in the snow for traditional cross-country skiers and/or groomed flat for the aerobically demanding activity called skating. Instruction and rental equipment are readily available. Many Alpine ski resorts and some dude ranches also set up cross-country facilities and programs as optional activities.

But controlled, patrolled cross-country trails are only a part of the Colorado Nordic scene. As you drive along snow-banked highways throughout the Colorado Rockies on a winter weekend, you'll see cars and pickups parked in pull-outs all along the way. It's not that Colorado vehicles have the worst breakdown rate in the West. It's more that Colorado is a big backcountry skiing state, and those pull-outs serve as official or impromptu trailheads. Skiers follow routes through the woods on what in summer are hiking trails, four-wheel-drive routes, old railroad beds, or high pass roads that are closed in winter. The rewards for taking the offbeat paths are sensational views or sensational powder runs through untracked snow.

The popularity of backcountry skiing and the growing sophistication of equipment has spurred a renaissance of telemarking. This elegant free-heel style of skiing has its origins in the early days of skiing in Scandinavia, and while you'll see telemarkers at ski areas all over Colorado, purists

213

still prefer laying first tracks in a backcountry powder field they've worked to reach.

For many outdoor enthusiasts, the epitome of winter is an expedition that takes several days. The long-cherished European tradition of skiing through high mountains and overnighting in huts has taken root in Colorado, with several systems of extensive backcountry trails and huts or yurts along the way. Colorado's oldest hut group is the Alfred A. Braun Memorial System between Aspen and Crested Butte, but the largest and most famous is the Tenth Mountain Division Trail System, which laces through a huge area surrounding the Holy Cross Wilderness between Aspen and Vail. Created by visionary Aspen architect Fritz Benedict and a group of volunteers, this network was envisioned for winter, has steadily gained in popularity, and is now open for hiking and mountain biking in summer as well as for skiing in winter. Several other systems now have also been developed.

Another way to explore the backcountry is on snow-shoes, an activity that combines winter sport, recreational activity, and fitness. Or you can also hook up with a team of huskies and cross the snow on a sled, which lets the canines enjoy their traditional winter sport, recreational activity (they do love to run!), and fitness technique. Touring and mountaineering gear and snowshoes are available for rent at outdoor stores all over Colorado.

TYPES OF NORDIC SKIING

In classic cross-country skiing, the skier uses thin, light-weight skis and low-cut boots to glide along tracks etched several inches into the snow. Waxless skis, which require no base preparation, are popular with recreational skiers. The basic technique is a stride accompanied by poling, with arms and legs in opposition, just like walking. This traditional form of skiing is also called diagonal skiing. In recent years, ski manufacturers have developed short skis, which are easier to master. Cross-country centers groom and track-set large networks of this type of trail. Many sections are double-tracked, meaning that there are two sets of parallel tracks to provide a passing lane. Sometimes outlying trails are marked but not groomed, and backcountry trails are always left that way. Recently, fitness fanatics have become enamored of a newer Nordic skill, which is called skating because that's what it resembles. Skaters use long poles, special skating skis, and an immense amount of energy to propel themselves along flat lanes of packed snow by pushing off with the inside edges of their skis and poling. Backcountry skiers often use sturdier, heavier equipment—often including skis with full or partial metal edges that can be used for telemarking—suitable for the variable conditions found off the groomed trails.

Backcountry skiing is the winter version of hiking, and in fact many of the same trails that hikers use in the warm months are converted for skiing in the cold, snowy ones. The next extension of backcountry skiing is the overnight trip. Hut-to-hut and, more recently, yurt-to-yurt excursions with or without a guide are increasingly popular in Colorado, but the hardiest types load their packs with four-season tents, subzero sleeping bags, and other equipment for winter camping. Mountaineering skis, plus an array of winter-survival accessories, are a necessity for those making long winter-camping expeditions.

Telemark skiing resembles a cross between Nordic and Alpine skiing. The equipment approaches Alpine gear in

terms of heft and performance capabilities, but the bindings allow for free-heel skiing. It is the technique required
for backcountry skiing, but it can also be used at a lift-
served Alpine area. Although telemarkers abound at
Colorado's Alpine ski areas, telemarking is generally
taught at Nordic ski schools.

WHERE TO SKI

Both new and experienced cross-country skiers find
Colorado's myriad cross-country centers ideal for a few
days on the track. The centers offer miles of marked and
mostly track-set trails for skiers of different ability levels,
groomed skating lanes, instruction, rentals, cafeterias or
other food services, and one or two trailside warming huts.
Unless indicated otherwise, expect to pay a modest trail
fee. Many of the ski schools offer guided track and backcountry skiing as well as traditional lessons. A free
brochure listing many of Colorado's top Nordic centers is
available from:
Colorado Cross Country Ski Association
P.O. Box 1336
Winter Park, CO 80482
800-869-4560

CROSS-COUNTRY CENTERS, TRAIL SYSTEMS, AND OTHER DETAILS

Adventures to the Edge
P.O. Box 91
707 Elk Avenue
Crested Butte, CO 81224
800-349-5219, 970-349-5219

Half- and full-day tours around Crested Butte, with fondue
dinner option in a hut; peak ascents and descents on skis;
guided hut trips

Ashcroft Touring Center
Castle Creek Road
Aspen, CO 81612
970-925-1971
35 kilometers of trails from an old mining town

Aspen and Snowmass
Aspen Nordic Council
P.O. Box 10815
Aspen, CO 81612
970-925-2145
80 kilometers of trails within a 15-mile area, including the
Owl Creek Trail between Aspen and Snowmass; no trail fee

Beaver Creek Touring Center
P.O. Box 81657
Vail, CO 81657
970-949-5750
32 kilometers of mountaintop trails at McCoy Park, accessible via high-speed chairlift with slow loading and unloading
areas

Beaver Meadows
P.O. Box 178
Red Feather Lakes, CO 80543
800-462-5870, 970-881-2450
25 kilometers of trails

Breckenridge Nordic Center
P.O. Box 1776
1200 Ski Hill Road
Breckenridge, CO 80424
970-453-6855
28 kilometers of trails

Copper Mountain Cross Country Center
P.O. Box 3001
Copper Mountain, CO 80443
800-458-8386, Ext. 5;
970-968-2882, Ext. 6342
25 kilometers of trails

Crested Butte Nordic Center
620 Second Street
Crested Butte, CO 81225
970-349-1707
30 kilometers of trails; in-town location; clearinghouse for
backcountry tours

Devil's Thumb
P.O. Box 1364
Winter Park, CO 80482
970-726-8231
85 kilometers of trails

Eldora Nordic Center
P.O. Box 1378
Nederland, CO 80406
303-440-8700
45 kilometers of trails

Frisco Nordic Ski Center
P.O. Box 532
Colorado State Highway 9
Frisco, CO 80443
970-668-0866
35 kilometers of trails

Grand Lake Touring Center
P.O. Box 590
Grand Lake, CO 80447
970-627-8008
20 kilometers of trails

Keystone Cross Country Center
P.O. Box 38
Keystone, CO 80435
800-451-5930, Ext. 4275;
970-468-4275
29 kilometers of groomed trails, plus 29 kilometers of back-country trails; access to mountaintop trails by gondola

Piney Creek Nordic Center
P.O. Box 896
Leadville, CO 80461
719-486-1750
25 kilometers of trails; North America's highest Nordic center, with all trails above 10,000 feet; located at Ski Cooper

SilverCreek Nordic Center
P.O. Box 1110
SilverCreek, CO 80446
800-448-9458, 970-887-3384,
303-629-1020 (metro Denver)

40 kilometers of trails connected with 50 kilometers at adjacent Snow Mountain Ranch, skiable on one ticket

Ski Sunlight Nordic Center
10901 County Road 117
Glenwood Springs, CO 81601
800-445-7931, 970-945-7491
10 kilometers of trails; no trail fee

Snow Mountain Ranch Nordic Center
P.O. Box 169
Winter Park, CO 80482
970-887-2152
50 kilometers of trails connected with 40 kilometers at adjacent SilverCreek, skiable on one trail pass

Steamboat Ski Touring Center
P.O. Box 772297
Steamboat Springs, CO 80477
970-879-8180
30 kilometers of trails

Telluride Nordic
P.O. Box 11155
595 Mountain Village Boulevard
Telluride, CO 81435
970-728-7545
10 kilometers of valley trails for beginners and intermediates and mountain trails accessed by chairlift

Twin Lakes
Twin Lakes Nordic Inn

6435 State Highway 82
Twin Lakes, CO 81251
800-748-2317, 719-486-1830
About a dozen no-fee trails from the old stage stop of Twin Lakes. Ranging from easy two-miler to demanding 11-mile climb (and 11-mile return) to the top of Independence Pass; no trail fee

DUDE RANCHES

Many of the dude and guest ranches that are open in winter offer some form of cross-country skiing to their guests, but the following have particularly strong Nordic skiing facilities and programs:
C Lazy U Ranch
P.O. Box 379
Granby, CO 80446
970-887-3344
25 kilometers of trails

The Home Ranch Resort
P.O. Box 822
Clark, CO 80428
970-879-9044
40 kilometers of trails

Latigo Ranch
P.O. Box 237
Kremmling, CO 80459
800-227-9655
50 kilometers of trails

Vista Verde Guest Ranch
P.O. Box 465
Steamboat Springs, CO 81657
800-526-6433
30 kilometers of trails

FOREST SERVICE AND OTHER PUBLIC LANDS

Many leading hiking areas are also outstanding for Nordic skiing. Routes may be wide, easy-to-follow roads or narrow trails marked with small colored flags or painted blazes on the trees. The trails will not be groomed, so even a short trip offers an introduction to the technical flexibility required for backcountry skiing and the equipment that will make it easier. Special Nordic-skiing or winter-recreation maps are also useful. For information on some recommended areas for skiing, including Rocky Mountain National Park, national forests, wilderness areas, and state parks, see the "Where to Hike" section of the "Afoot" chapter.

HUT AND YURT SYSTEMS

A network of high-country lodgings makes the backcountry accessible to most reasonably fit Nordic skiers. Huts have their roots in the Alps, but in the Rockies, their styles range from simple cottages and A-frames to relatively lavish log structures. Yurts, derived from Mongolian dwellings, are round, tent-like structures built on platforms. The hut or yurt will probably be equipped with tables, benches that also may be used as sleeping platforms, mattresses or pads, a stove and cooking equipment, firewood, and electric lighting, and there will probably be a privy. You must bring in your own sleeping bag, food, and personal gear. Reservations are mandatory and should be made well in advance for weekends and full moons because few mountain scenes are as romantic as those where lunar light illuminates the snowy landscape.

Alfred A. Braun Memorial Hut System
c/o Tenth Mountain Division Hut
System (see below)
Six huts in the Elk Mountains

Hinsdale Haute Route
P.O. Box 771
Lake City, CO 81235
970-944-2269
Colorado's newest system, with two yurts in the San Juan Mountains

Mountain Creek Ranch
P.O. Box 134
Jefferson, CO 80456
970-789-1834
Packed trails on ranch property plus Homestead Cabin and two backcountry yurts in Pike National Forest

Never Summer Nordic Yurts
P.O. Box 1983
Fort Collins, CO 80522
970-482-9411
Four yurts in Colorado State Forest

San Juan Hut Systems
P.O. Box 1663
Telluride, CO 81435
970-728-6935
Four huts in the San Juans between Telluride and Ridgway

Summit Huts & Trails Association
c/o Tenth Mountain Division Hut System (see below)
Two cabins with links to the Tenth Mountain Division
system

Tenth Mountain Division Hut System
1280 Ute Avenue
Aspen, CO 81611
970-925-5775
300 miles of intermittently marked trails; 17 huts in White
River and San Isabel National Forests; also acts as a reservations service for the Braun and Summit huts

GUIDED BACKCOUNTRY SKIING

In addition to these guide services, which specialize in
backcountry ski tours, some hiking guides also lead winter
treks on request. (See the "Afoot" chapter)

OUTFITTERS, AREA, AND OTHER DETAILS

Backcountry Ski Guides
P.O. Box 866
Winter Park, CO 80482
970-726-4812

Ski tours, avalanche seminars, intro to backcountry and winter camping courses in Arapaho National Forest

Paragon Guides
P.O. Box 130
Vail, CO 81658
970-926-5299
Three- to six-day itineraries using the Tenth Mountain Division Trail and Hut System

San Juan Hut Systems (see above)
Guided day and multi-day trips

Shrine Mountain Adventure
P.O. Box 4
Red Cliff, CO 81649
970-827-5363
Beginner and intermediate tours; weekly Shrine Pass tours

SNOWSHOEING

Snowshoes are the sports-utility vehicles of the winter backcountry. They go through tight spots where cross-country skis won't, keep you atop the snow where feet would sink deep, and generally make lighter work of maneuvering. Snowshoeing is growing in popularity as a valid activity unto itself, and many hikers and backpackers now routinely strap a pair on their packs in case they encounter deep snow in the fall or spring.

Nicknamed "the quiet sport," snowshoeing is also the ideal way to explore mountain forests in a tranquil way. While snowshoeing is astonishingly easy to learn (hint: it's easier with ski poles than without), independent wilderness travel requires the normal cautions. Many Colorado cross-country centers and Alpine ski areas now welcome snow-shoers, and some, such as Vail and Beaver Creek Nordic Centers (970-845-5313), offer guided snowshoe tours as well as rentals. Another option is to take a naturalist tour or guided snowshoe adventure led by a park ranger at Rocky Mountain National Park (970-586-2371), by a private guide, or by a guide from another organization, such as one of the following:

GUIDE SERVICE, AREA, AND OTHER DETAILS

Adventures to the Edge
P.O. Box 91
707 Elk Avenue
Crested Butte, CO 81224
800-349-5219, 970-349-5219

Aspen Center for Environmental Studies
(ACES)
P.O. Box 877
Aspen, CO 81612
970-925-5756
Naturalist tours from the top of Aspen Mountain

Bigfoot Snowshoe Tours
P.O. Box 1010
Nederland, CO 80466
303-258-3157
(Reservations also through Mountain Sports, 303-443-6770, or the Inn at Nederland, 800-279-9463)
Roosevelt National Forest

Chuck McGuire Outdoors
P.O. Box 703
Vail, CO 81658
970-949-0955
Custom tours for groups of four to seven to Adam's Rib
Ranch

Rocky Mountain National Park
Estes Park, CO 80517
970-586-1223
Ranger-led walks from Bear Lake

Shrine Mountain Adventure
P.O. Box 4
Red Cliff, CO 81649
970-827-5363
Naturalist tours to Grouse Lake and Grouse Creek

Vail and Beaver Creek Nordic Centers
P.O. Box 7
Vail, CO 81657
970-845-5313
Various trails at and near Vail and Beaver Creek

DOGSLEDDING

Alaska's Iditarod has given dogsledding a great mystique
as the ultimate winter adventure, but in its milder forms, it
is an enchanting activity for the casual participant. The famous old television series "Sergeant Preston of the Yukon"

was actually filmed in Colorado, near Ashcroft. The Toklat kennels established near that ghost town above Aspen became the genesis for mushing in Colorado. Krabloonik in nearby Snowmass is the state's largest and most famous sled-dog kennel, but several operators now offer dogsled excursions. On some, you are just a passenger, taking a ride in the sled as the musher handles the team that pulls you across the snow. Others will teach guests the rudiments of mushing, which doesn't take all that long to learn but does require a willingness and an ability to run behind the sled at husky pace, or at least ride one runner while pedaling with the free foot. Outings may be just an hour or two, with or without lunch, but some outfitters also can arrange a wilderness camping expedition by dogsled. For general information on mushing, contact:

Colorado Mountain Mushers Association
8931 South Hillview Road
Morrison, CO 80465
303-697-4071, 303-934-7246

In addition, several terrific races and other great spectator events dot the winter calendar. The annual Granby Sled Dog Classic is held late in January or early in February; the Grand Lake Area Chamber of Commerce (970-627-3402) has the dates. The Gold Mush is part of Frisco's Gold Rush festivities, generally in the last half of February; for exact dates, call the Town of Frisco (800-424-1554, 970-668-5276). The annual Defiance Sled Dog Race takes place in Four Mile Park near Glenwood Springs in mid-March; details are available from the Glenwood Springs Chamber Resort Association (800-221-0098, 970-945-6589).

OUTFITTERS

Good Times Tours
P.O. Box 68
Frisco, CO 80443
800-477-0144, 970-453-7604, 970-668-0930

Krabloonik Kennels
P.O. Box 5517
Snowmass Village, CO 81615
970-923-4342, 970-923-3953

Lucky Cat Dog Farm
900 County Road 13
Gunnison, CO 81230
970-641-1636

The Mountain Musher
P.O. Box 1386
Eagle, CO 81631
970-328-7877

Wolf Canyon Mushers
P.O. Box 2051
Eagle, CO 81631
970-328-6930

TIPS FOR WINTER IN THE BACKCOUNTRY

The winter wilderness can be a magical place, but the environment is not to be taken lightly. To avoid dehydration, drink water before you are thirsty. To avoid hypothermia, be sure to stay warm and dry with proper perspiration-wicking clothing and layering. To avoid frostbite, be sure to keep your extremities warm with warm socks and gloves and bring goggles and a neck gaiter or warm scarf to protect your face from cold winds.

Avalanches

In addition to all these cautions, it cannot be stated too strongly that the single most significant danger of winter in the backcountry is the avalanche potential, and the most important advice for traveling through the backcountry in winter is to be alert for avalanches. Unless a group travels exclusively in areas known to be slide-safe, someone in the group needs to be competent in analyzing avalanche potential, and all group members should understand and practice rescue techniques. Guides are extensively trained in avalanche safety, so the best bet for backcountry novices is to go with an organized group. Frequently updated avalanche information is available through the winter from the following hotline numbers:

Colorado Avalanche Information Center	303-371-1080
Aspen (Pitkin County)	970-920-1664
Colorado Springs	719-520-0020
Denver/Boulder	303-275-5360
Dillon (Summit County)	970-668-0600
Durango	970-247-8187
Fort Collins	970-482-0457
Minturn (Eagle County, Vail area)	970-827-5687

Rating System

A system of avalanche ratings, similar to the reports on road or ski conditions, has been developed for the back-country. They do not apply to developed ski areas, where avalanche control measures are used. Condition reports should act as a potent guide to if, where, and when to go. The most commonly used rating system follows:

Low: Mostly stable snow. Avalanches are unlikely except in isolated pockets on steep snow-covered open slopes and gullies.

Moderate: Areas of unstable snow. Avalanches are possible on steep, snow-covered open slopes and gullies.

High: Mostly unstable snow. Avalanches are likely on steep, snow-covered slopes and gullies.

Extreme: Widespread areas of unstable snow. Avalanches are certain on some steep snow-covered slopes and gullies. Large destructive avalanches are possible.

Avalanche Awareness

This is not meant to be more than the most cursory overview of what to be alert for in the backcountry. Nothing can substitute for a qualified guide or experienced backcountry traveler with specialized training. But in general, remember that most avalanches are triggered by people. Carry and know how to use an avalanche rescue transceiver or beacon, a shovel, and a collapsible snow probe. Even backcountry veterans make occasional errors in judgment, but these can be minimized by learning to detect nature's clues and approaching the backcountry with respect and caution.

Most avalanches occur during and shortly after storms, when winds carry snow and deposit it on the lee or sheltered sides of mountains, ridges, and gullies. Snowfall of twelve inches or more in twenty-four hours can lead to unstable conditions. Since cold air does not allow new snow to settle and stabilize, backcountry adventurers should be aware of sudden and drastic weather changes that can further destabilize snow. Because avalanches are most common on slopes of thirty to forty-five degrees, be suspicious of snow-loaded leeward slopes and avoid traveling on or under cornices. Trees, boulders, and rock outcrops help anchor snow only until they become buried, since open slopes allow snow to slide. While tree-covered slopes are generally the safest, avalanches can also occur there. Be alert to open slopes between vegetated areas and look for bent or broken trees and branches that are broken off of the uphill side of the trunk, indicating that avalanches have occurred there. The safest areas are generally on the windward side of ridges and in valleys.

Further signs of recent avalanche activity include wind-blown snow, smooth "pillows," cornices, and drifted areas. Listen for drum-like sounds from the snow and look for cracks shooting out in the snow. These all indicate an unstable snowpack. If you must cross hazardous terrain, travel on the windward side of ridges or stay in valley floors away from steep hillsides. As much as possible, stay in tree-covered areas. Avoid such "terrain traps" as cliffs, gullies, and short, steep leeward slopes. Do not assume that an area is safe because someone else has previously crossed it. Stay in a group, but never travel close together in avalanche country. Before crossing a suspicious area, tuck in loose clothing, remove ski-pole straps from your wrists and ski safety straps from your legs, loosen your backpack shoulder straps and release the waist belt, because loose equipment can drag you down if you are caught in an avalanche. Cross the potential avalanche area one person at a time. Move quickly across a steep snow-covered slope and head for a safe location such as large outcroppings and tree islands.

Avalanche courses are offered by numerous climbing schools, outdoor-education programs, and the Colorado Mountain Club (see the Afoot chapter), but an especially ambitious curriculum of hands-on backcountry avalanche and rescue courses, ranging from winter survival skills to mountain-guide courses, is offered by:

Adventures to the Edge
P.O. Box 91
Crested Butte, CO 81224
800-349-5219, 970-349-5219

What to Bring

When skiing or snowshoeing at a controlled, patrolled cross-country center, you'll need little more than warm, nonbulky clothing that allows easy movement, gloves or mittens, head protection, sunglasses and/or goggles, sunscreen, and your own equipment or rental gear. As in an Alpine ski area, it is easy to purchase or rent whatever you might be missing. When venturing into the backcountry, however, even for a day, take what you would for track skiing plus extra clothing for layering, gaiters to keep the unpacked snow out of your boots, spare gloves and/or glove liners, spare socks, sufficient water, energy snacks, an insulated container with a hot beverage, a strong sun-block, and a first-aid kit, and add all the other parapher-nalia you'd take on a long hike (maps, compass, altimeter, etc.; see the "Afoot" chapter).

Disposable heat packs for gloves and boots are a com-fort extra that can also help prevent frostbite. If you are going on a hut or yurt trip, you'll also need extra water, food, a sleeping bag, a flashlight, some emergency ski-repair materials, a spare ski-pole basket, a lighter and/or waterproof matches, a bivouac sack, and equipment for contingencies, such as ski poles that can be converted to avalanche probes, lightweight shovels, or even rescue transceivers, for some situations. (It is even wise to bring some of these items for an arduous day of skiing or a snow-shoe tour.)

What Not to Bring

If you are hut- or yurt-skiing, leave your dog at home, because canines are not permitted in most backcountry lodgings.

READING LIST

The Avalanche Book by Betsy Armstrong and Knob Williams (Fulcrum Publishing, 350 Indiana Street, Golden, CO 80401)
Colorado Hut to Hut by Brian Litz (Westcliffe Publishers, Inc., 2650 South Zuni Street, Englewood, CO 80110)
Colorado Mountain Ski Tours and Hikes by Dave Mueller

(Quality Press, DAM Enterprises, P.O. Box 61332, Denver, CO 80206)

Skiing Colorado's Backcountry by Brian Litz (Fulcrum Publishing)

Snowshoeing by Gene Prater (The Mountaineers, 1011 S.W. Klickitat Way, Suite 107, Seattle, WA 98134)

11
IN A STREAM

Colorado is a year-round fishing state, with abundant waters that attract adherents to every form of the sport, from fly-fishing for wild trout, to underwater spearfishing for carp in lakes, to ice-fishing in the short days of winter. With the poetry of motion and symbolism displayed in the film *A River Runs Through It*, Western fly-fishing has assumed nearly mythic proportions, and, in fact, John Dietsch, who supervised the film's fly-fishing scenes, is a Colorado fly-fishing guide.

Fly-fishing provides a connection to primal instincts and emotions. The ceaseless flow of the river, where wild fish hatch, grow, breed, and die, is a clear metaphor for the continuity of life itself. Creating—or at least selecting—the proper fly for the day offers the satisfaction of knowing we can fool a creature as primitive as a fish, and it humbles us when we are outsmarted instead. The strike of a trout on the line, and the brief battle to catch it, reflects many of life's challenges, and the act of reeling it in, admiring its shimmering beauty, and returning it to the stream is oddly nurturing. Symbolism aside, it's an activity that is at once thrilling, challenging, and relaxing.

In addition to its wondrous steams and rivers, Colorado's lakes and reservoirs present a different fishing environment as well as different species of fish. Fishing from a boat, canoe, or inflatable can be incredibly relaxing, and it is especially suitable for families with small children or anyone not interested in or able to negotiate stream banks and moving water. Many of the larger lakes have boat-rental facilities and launch ramps. Shore-fishing, arguably one of the most down-home of all outdoor activities, can also provide successful fishing in many bodies of water.

Like most of Colorado's outdoor activities, fishing owes its quality to the mountains. Snowfall, snowmelt, and its subsequent runoff combine to create exceptional opportunities in the more than 65,000 miles of streams and over 2,000 lakes and reservoirs from the plains to high mountain cirques that are open to public fishing.

COLORADO SPORT FISH

Popular cold-water sport fish include brown trout, rainbow trout, native cutthroat trout, brook trout, kokanee salmon, lake trout (mackinaw), and mountain whitefish. Warm-water species include white crappie, channel catfish, walleye, yellow perch, tiger muskie, bluegill, largemouth bass, smallmouth bass, white bass, and wiper. The native cutthroat, the only trout species not introduced to local waters by humans, is now found primarily in high mountain streams in the Colorado River drainage, and fishing for it is presently restricted to catch-and-release fishing using artificial lures in rivers designated as cutthroat recovery waters. The largest fish recorded caught in Colorado was a thirty-three-pound, four-ounce channel catfish, a native species often successfully caught at night. The Colorado squawfish, boneytail, humpback cub, and razorback sucker have been declared endangered fish in the Upper Colorado River Basin.

To accommodate fishing pressure, there is an aggressive "put-and-take" management approach in most Colorado waters. The state's sixteen fish hatcheries raise and stock more than eighteen million cold-water fish and seventy-one million warm-water fish, which means that officials put fish in and anglers pull them out. Additionally, selected streams are managed to produce wild trout and are therefore not stocked with hatchery fish. Dedicated fishermen view these as higher-quality fish, with better color, more genetic variety, and more fight. The Colorado Division of Wildlife (address below) has details. Because natural run-off varies from spring through fall and since many rivers are controlled, water levels can vary greatly. To obtain stream-flow information, see the "Paddle Power" chapter.

COLORADO FISHING REGULATIONS AND PRACTICES

The state sets fishing-season and water regulations every three years, with the next slated for 1996. At this writing, all Colorado waters are open to the taking of all but endangered species, except as limited in specific rivers, streams, and lakes. Size, bag, and possession limits vary by species and location, but catch-and-release fishing using barbless hooks is preferred by those who fish for diversion and sport. Fish must be returned alive to the waters from which they are taken. Anglers over sixteen years of age must have a valid license to fish in public waters (with certain active and retired military personnel exempted). Regular resident, nonresident, and senior-resident licenses for those sixty-four or older are available from fly and tackle shops and outfitters throughout the state. The first full weekend in June is currently an annual free fishing weekend, during which license requirements are waived.

Of Colorado's 8,000-plus miles of trout streams, only 158 bear Gold Medal designation. In order to maintain their quality, they may be governed by special regulations that allow only flies and lures to be used and often mandate only catch-and-release fishing. Since only the best of the best are Gold Medal Waters, so honored by the Colorado Division of Wildlife for their excellent populations of large trout, it is in the interest of all to maintain this quality.

Recorded fishing information, updated weekly from April 1 through September 30 and approximately on a monthly basis the rest of the year, is available from the following numbers:

General information	303-291-7533
Stocking report	303-291-7531
Metro Denver and Foothills	303-291-7535
Northeastern Colorado	303-291-7536
Northwestern Colorado	303-291-9537
Southeastern Colorado	303-291-7538
Southwestern Colorado	303-291-7539

Fishing regulations vary greatly. In streams, there are issues of access, size and bag limits, and lures. Many lakes and reservoirs are zoned, with fishing and other uses permitted or prohibited in certain areas. Additional restrictions regulate access season (some are completely off-limits during the migratory waterfowl season), the types of craft permitted (motorized or not), and whether night fishing is permitted. Anglers are urged to contact individual regulatory agencies. In addition, the following areas permit fishing under their own regulations and restrictions:

Fort Carson Military Reservation
Environment, Energy & Natural Resources Office
Colorado Springs, CO 80913
719-579-2752

Rocky Mountain National Park
Estes Park, CO 80517
970-586-2371

Southern Ute Reservation
P.O. Box 737
Ignacio, CO 81137
970-563-4525, Ext. 417

Ute Mountain Ute Reservation
Towaoc, CO 81334
970-565-3751

Many anglers need only themselves and their gear for an exceptional day of fishing. But with their knowledge of the state's waters and the proper flies, lures, or bait for the season, specialty outfitters and fishing guides virtually guarantee success, and they can always provide a tip or two. In addition, with or without a guide, fishing is easily combinable with other outdoor pursuits. Increasingly popular with anglers are float trips, where the guide maneuvers a raft or a McKenzie River boat down a scenic river that offers a changing selection of coves and eddies and a longer drift to each cast. Fishing and rafting outfitters often cross services, too, with fishing guides offering the float option, and many raft outfitters also organizing float trips (see the "Afloat" chapter). Fishing is also a natural to combine with hiking, backpacking, camping, or horsepacking. Private fishing lodges with their own lakes, ponds, and stretches of flowing water require no licenses. These are not included here.

WHERE TO FISH

Close to Denver, the best fishing can be found in Aurora Reservoir, Chatfield Reservoir, Cherry Creek Reservoir, Quincy Reservoir, the South Platte River, and Evergreen Creek/Bear Creek. The state's record tiger muskie, weighing in at twenty-seven pounds, was pulled from Quincy Reservoir. In the northern Front Range, the Big Thompson and the Cache La Poudre, which begin in Rocky Mountain National Park, offer excellent trout fishing (brown, native, rainbow, and some mountain whitefish). Three sections of the Poudre are restricted to fly- and lure-fishing.

Colorado's mountain rivers and streams are productive and picturesque. Flowing through scenery so magnificent that it makes the eyeballs ache, the Arkansas, Blue, Crystal, Dolores, Fryingpan, Gunnison, Illinois, Michigan, Norris Creek, North Platte, Rio Grande, Roaring Fork, and Taylor Rivers cascade from the central and western mountains and all offer excellent fishing. Among the reservoirs, Blue Mesa, Dillon, McPhee, Rifle Gap, and Taylor, plus

Steamboat and Sweetwater Lakes and the lakes and reservoirs on Grand Mesa, offer prime flat-water fishing. Vallecito Lake, northwest of Durango, has state records for northern pike (thirty pounds, one ounce; 48.25 inches long) and German brown trout (twenty-four pounds, ten ounces; 37.5 inches long). Campgrounds are on or near most reservoirs and lakes, but regulations regarding motorized boats vary.

Parts of the Blue River, Colorado River, Fryingpan River, Gore Creek, Gunnison River, North Delaney Butte Lake, North Platte River, Rio Grande, Roaring Fork River, middle and south forks of the South Platte River, and Spinney Mountain Reservoir currently bear Gold Medal Waters designation, giving them instant cachet with anglers. The Blue River, Cache La Poudre River, Cascade Creek, Cochetopa Creek, Colorado River, Conejos Reservoir, East River, Emerald Lakes, Fraser River, Gunnison River, Lake Fork of the Conejos, Laramie River, Los Pinos Creek, North Platte River, North St. Vrain Creek, Osier Creek, Roaring Fork River, South Platte River, middle fork of the South Platte River, Tarryall Creek, and Trappers Lake are wild-trout waters that support self-sustaining populations and are stocked only under emergency circumstances. The longest stretch is thirty-four miles of the Blue River from the Dillon Reservoir Dam to the confluence with the Colorado River. These rivers are renowned for their populations of spirited, quality fish that serious anglers treasure beyond their hatchery-raised kin.

In contrast to the dramatic mountains, the expansive plains of eastern Colorado have little allure for most outdoor enthusiasts. Anglers are the exception, and those who favor this part of this state treasure the variety of fish they can find in the state's eastern waters. Tiger muskie, bass, saugeye, crappie, walleye, wiper, and catfish are abundant in the reservoirs in the lower Arkansas River Valley, Bonny Reservoir, and Trinidad Reservoir in the southeast, while the three Delaney Butte Lakes and Cowdrey Lake in the northeast are considered prime for various species of trout.

Fishing doesn't end when the snow falls. Several outfitters specialize in winter fly-fishing, and ice-fishing on frozen lakes and reservoirs is a cult of its own. Ice-fishing is best at Antero Reservoir, Aurora Reservoir, Blue Mesa Reservoir, Chatfield Reservoir, Elevenmile Reservoir, Granby Reservoir, Georgetown Reservoir, Lake John, Stagecoach Reservoir, Steamboat Lake, and Taylor Reservoir.

Fishing maps, specialized brochures and books, and a comprehensive guide called the *Colorado Fishing Season Information and Wildlife Property Directory*, which includes land- and water-use regulations and a detailed listing of waters, are available from:
Colorado Division of Wildlife
Department of Natural Resources
6060 Broadway
Denver, CO 80216
303-297-1192

OUTFITTERS

Outfitters and fishing guides offer services from beginner fly-casting instruction to multi-day float trips to Colorado's remotest and most productive waters. Many outfitters, guides, and fly-fishing schools also teach fly tying, the arcane skill of creating artificial lures that "match the catch."

All Seasons Ranch
P.O. Box 252
Craig, CO 81626
970-824-4526

Aspen Trout Guides at Pomeroy Sports
414 East Durant Street
Aspen, CO 81612
970-920-1050, 970-925-7875

Berfield's High Mountain Drifters
211 East Tomichi Avenue
Gunnison, CO 81230
800-793-4243, 970-641-4243

Buggywhip's Fish & Float Service
P.O. Box 770477
Steamboat Springs, CO 80477
800-759-0343, 970-879-8033

Columbine Outfitters
Fifth & Main Streets
Frisco, CO 80443
970-668-3704
and
191 Blue River Parkway
Silverthorne, CO 80498
970-262-0966

Columbine School of Flyfishing
516 Park Avenue
Salida, CO 81201
719-539-3136

Creative Sports
P.O. Box 775247
Steamboat Springs, CO 80477
970-879-1568, 970-879-0884

Don's Fly Shop
P.O. Box 220
Lake City, CO 81235
970-944-2281

Echo Canyon Outfitters
P.O. Box 328
La Veta, CO 81055
719-742-5524 (day), 719-742-5403 (evening)

Estes Angler
338 West Riverside Drive
Estes Park, CO 80517
970-586-2110

Fly Fishing Outfitters
P.O. Box 2861
Vail, CO 81658
970-476-FISH

Gore Creek Fly Fisherman
183 Gore Creek Drive
Vail, CO 81657
970-476-3296

Hawkins Outfitters
692 County Road 46
Howard, CO 81233
719-942-3393

Chuck McGuire Flyfishing
174 East Gore Creek Drive
P.O. Box 703
Vail, CO 81658
970-476-1301 (Vail), 970-949-0955 (Beaver Creek)

Monarch Guides
P.O. Box 967
Kremmling, CO 80459
800-882-3445, 970-653-4210

Monarch Guides & Outfitters
P.O. Box 255
Gypsum, CO 81637
800-882-3445 (May 15 to September 15), 970-524-7444
    (year-round)

Mountain Man Tours
Box 11, Eagles Nest
Creede, CO 81130
719-658-2663 (May to October), 719-658-2843 (year-round)

Nelson's Fishing Guide
P.O. Box 336
Tabernash, CO 80478
970-726-8558

Nova Guides
P.O. Box 2018
Vail, CO 81658
970-949-4232

Olympic Sports/Orvis Fly Fishing
150 West Colorado Avenue
Telluride, CO 81435
800-828-7547, 970-728-4477

Oxbow Outfitting Co.
675 East Durant Street
P.O. Box D-3
Aspen, CO 81612
800-421-1505, 970-925-1505 (Aspen)
800-247-2755, 970-923-5959 (Snowmass)

Roaring Fork Anglers
2022 Grand Avenue
Glenwood Springs, CO 81601
970-945-0180

Scot's Sporting Goods
U.S. 36
Estes Park, CO 80517
970-586-2877

Steamboat Lake Fishing
P.O. Box 990
Clark, CO 80428
800-332-1889, 303-879-3045

Straightline Fly & Tackle
744 Lincoln Avenue
P.O. Box 774887
Steamboat Springs, CO 80477
800-354-5463, 970-879-7568

Jackson Streit's Mountain Angler
P.O. Box 467
311 South Main Street
Breckenridge, CO 80424
970-453-HOOK

Summit Guides
P.O. Box 2489
Dillon, CO 80435
970-468-8945

Sundance Fly Fishing
P.O. Box 2673
Telluride, CO 81435
970-728-6995

Taylor Creek Mountain Anglers
Basalt City Market Shopping Center
Basalt, CO 81621
970-927-4374 (Basalt), 970-920-1128 (Aspen)

Telluride Outside Fly Fishing
P.O. Box 685
666 West Colorado Avenue
Telluride, CO 81435
800-831-6230, 970-728-3895

Three Rivers Resort & Outfitting
P.O. Box 339
Almont, CO 81210
970-641-1303 (Almont), 970-349-5011 (Crested Butte)

In addition to the outfitters above, a list of licensed outfitters and guides is available from:
Colorado Department of Regulatory Agencies
1525 Sherman Street, #606
Denver, CO 80204
303-894-7778

FISHING FOR THE DISABLED

Chatfield Reservoir (303-791-7275) boasts some of the best accessible recreation in the metro Denver area, including a wheelchair-accessible fishing pier at Marina Point. For details on other accessible areas, contact Bonny State Recreation Area (970-354-7306), Cherry Creek Reservoir (303-699-3860), Colorado State Forest (970-723-8366), Dillon Reservoir (Dillon Ranger District, USFS, 970-468-5400), Golden Gate State Park (303-592-1502), Highline State Recreation Area (970-858-7208, 970-434-6862), Island Acres State Recreation Area (970-464-0548), Lathrop State Park (719-738-2376), Pike National Forest (Pikes Peak Ranger District, 719-636-1602), Pueblo State Recreation Area (719-561-9320), Trinidad State Recreation Area (719-846-6951), and Vega State Recreation Area (970-487-3407).

TIPS FOR ANGLERS

If you are fishing in restricted waters or simply prefer to "limit your kill" rather than "kill your limit," remember that fish that die after being caught and released do so more from stress than from injury. In order to return a healthy fish to the water, minimize out-of-water time, handle the fish minimally and only with wet hands or objects, carry an effective hook-removal tool, and remember that larger barbless hooks inflict less damage than smaller ones. If the fish is deeply hooked, cut the line to enhance the fish's chance of survival, and allow the fish to swim upstream when returning it gently to the water.

What to Bring

You'll need a valid Colorado fishing license, brimmed hat, sunscreen, insect repellent, fishing equipment (unless supplied by an outfitter or guide), rain gear, and warm jacket or sweater. Your father's old-style waders—rubber waders that resemble firefighters' boots on steroids—can be lethal if an angler falls and they fill with water. Today's Neoprene waders worn with felt-soled, antislip fishing shoes are far safer. Polarized sunglasses, preferably with retaining straps, are better than regular ones for spotting fish in the water. A camera, perhaps a waterproof disposable, is recommended for documenting the prize catches before they are released. Fishing gear can be rented from outfitters or tackle shops.

What Not to Bring

Avoid anything in a glass container, flimsy plastic bags, or other potential detritus that can wash downstream or fall into a reservoir or lake.

READING LIST

The Colorado Angling Guide by Chuck Fothergill and Bob
  Sterling (Stream Stalker Publishing, P.O. Box 238,
  Woody Creek, CO 81656)
Colorado Fishing Methods and Techniques (ML Publica-
  tions, P.O. Box 1682, Wheat Ridge, CO 80034)
*Colorado Lakes and Reservoirs Outdoor Recreational
  Guide* edited by Jack O. Olofson (Outdoor Books, P.O.
  Box 417, Denver, CO 80201)
Colorado Trout Fishing (ML Publications)
Fishing Close to Home (ML Publications)
The Front Range Lake Bottom Book (ML Publications)
Rocky Mountain Trout Fishing (ML Publications)

12

IN THE AIR

Those who want to get really high on the mountains can join the Colorado recreational air force. Hot-air balloons, small airplanes, sailplanes and gliders, helicopters for sightseeing, hang gliders, and ultralights are based all over the state. Each form of flight has its own magic, and each is enhanced by the surrounding mountains.

HOT-AIR BALLOONING

Hot-air balloons have gripped the human imagination since the days of the Montgolfier brothers and Jules Verne. Today, they are a staple of the Colorado recreational inventory. Ballooning ties the past to the present, and is ideal for celebrating a special event or viewing and photographing the mountains from a unique perspective. At once exciting and contemplative, recreational ballooning may not be able to take you "around the world in eighty days," but it can float you around the valley in an hour or two.

Balloon rides typically commence at daybreak, when a huge sack of colorful silk is inflated with hot air until it can lift a load of people into the sky. When all the passengers are on board, the balloon is released from its tethers and the peaceful thrill begins. The pilot manipulates the propane heater and otherwise fine-tunes the flight, but essentially, it is a ride on the air currents and feels like an effortless float. No other activity allows you to soar so easily on the wind, float across the landscape, and enjoy, literally, a bird's-eye view of mountains and valleys. Upon landing, the chase vehicle arrives to dispense champagne, and often breakfast, to guests while the crew packs the balloon and gets ready to ferry it and its passengers back to the starting point.

The traditional balloonist's prayer proffered as a champagne toast at the end of each flight is:

"May the wind welcome you with softness.

May the sun bless you with his warm hands.

May you fly so high and so well

That God will join you in laughter,

And set you gently back into the loving arms of
  Mother Earth."

After the flight, this simple sentiment has the power to touch believers and nonbelievers alike. Ballooning is a special-occasion indulgence everyone ought to sample— and if the "occasion" is a wonderful outdoor Colorado day, so much the better. "Aeronaut" is a another and quite delightful name for a balloonist, and being an aeronaut for a while is to be a member of an elite and romantic fellowship of the sky.

Balloon rides are not bargain amusements, so companies

253

are usually found in posh resorts. Flights generally are for one to two hours, with the exact takeoff determined by winds, not a fixed timetable. The pilot selects the altitude, which is usually several hundred feet above the ground. Since a balloon's only noise is the periodic surge of the propane flame, it is common to see wildlife as you sail by. Some operators welcome children from toddlers up; others prohibit children under six. If you prefer to partake of the unique ambience of ballooning without the expense, or what for many is a perceived risk, annual balloon festivals take place every summer at Snowmass and Steamboat Springs, and ballooning is a key element of the Thanksgiving High Flying Balloons and Bubbling Brew Fest in Breckenridge.

BALLOON RIDES

Adventures Aloft
P.O. Box 1085
Aspen, CO 81612
970-925-9497

Aero Sports Balloonists
P.O. Box 881891
Steamboat Plaza, CO 80488
970-879-7433

Balloon Adventures
704 White Rock
Crested Butte, CO 81224
970-349-6712

Balloon America
P.O. Box 604
Vail, CO 81657
970-HOT-AIRE

Balloons Out West
P.O. Box 38512
Colorado Springs, CO 80937
800-755-0935, 719-578-0935

Balloons Over Steamboat
P.O. Box 8830377
Steamboat Springs, CO 80488
970-879-3298

Big Horn Balloon Company
P.O. Box 361
Crested Butte, CO 81224
970-349-6335

Blue Sky Flying Adventures
P.O. Box 350
Granby, CO 80446
800-696-1384, 970-887-3001

Camelot Balloon
P.O. Box 1896
Vail, CO 81658
800-785-4743, 970-476-4743

High But Dry Balloons
P.O. Box 49006
Colorado Springs, CO 80949
800-393-3066, 719-260-0011

Life Cycle Balloon, Ltd.
2540 South Steele Street
Denver, CO 80210
303-759-3907

Pegasus Balloon Tours
P.O. Box 773462
Steamboat Springs, CO 80477
800-748-2487, 970-879-9191

San Juan Balloon Adventures
P.O. Box 66
Ridgway, CO 81432
970-626-5495

Unicorn Balloon Company of Colorado
300 AABC
Aspen, CO 81611
800-HOT-AIRS, 970-925-5752

Windwalker Tours
P.O. Box 775092
Steamboat Springs, CO 80477
800-748-1642, 970-879-8065

TIPS FOR AERONAUTS

The Federal Aviation Administration–licensed pilot does the work, so this is one outdoor adventure in which passengers are just that.

What to Bring

Be prepared to dress warmly for the season. Remember that it is always seasonally cold at first light as you're watching the balloon being inflated. Then, once in the air, passengers can't move around to keep warm in a balloon's open basket. In winter, it can be ten to thirty degrees warmer aloft than on the ground, since cold air settles. Dress as you would for a day of skiing. In summer, take clothing that can be layered and removed once the sun comes up. At any time of year, wear walking, hiking, or ahtletic footwear with warm socks. (Some operators prohibit sandals and open-toed shoes.) A camera and plenty of film are strongly recommended, though some balloon operators require you to get the pilot's clearance before bringing a video camera on board.

What Not to Bring

You won't need your fear of flying. Balloons look fragile, but they are resilient, the pilots are licensed and knowledgeable, and ballooning accidents are so rare that when they occur, they inevitably make big headlines and TV news bits, which create unnecessary worries. Leave your fears behind and enjoy the flight. Also, leave behind cigarettes, big bags, backpacks, and other bulky items, though some companies allow you to stow extra gear in the chase vehicle.

FLIGHTSEEING

Helicopters and fixed-wing aircraft lack the tranquillity of balloons, but they have a great range and for some people they are more familiar and offer more assurance. Glider rides combine the silence of ballooning with the security of sitting in a sailplane, which feels much like a small plane but with a light fuselage and long wings. Flight schools at small, general-aviation airports throughout the state will usually take passengers for tours, but the following companies specialize in that service.

AIRPLANES

Aspen Aviation
100 West Airport Road
Aspen, CO 81611
800-289-1369, 970-925-2522

Blue Sky Flying Adventures
P.O. Box 350
Granby, CO 80446
800-696-1384, 970-887-3001

Gunnison Valley Aviation
P.O. Box 834
1 Airport Road
Gunnison, CO 81230
970-641-0526

Leadville Air Tours
P.O. Box 1597

Leadville, CO 80461
719-486-2627

Salida Air Service
Harriet Alexander Field
9255 County Road 140
Salida, CO 81201
719-539-3720

Snowmass Aviation
P.O. Box 5406
Snowmass Village, CO 81615
970-923-2229

Steamboat Flying Service
P.O. Box 2168
Steamboat Springs, CO 80477
970-879-7427

HELICOPTERS

Colorado Copters
395 Airport Drive
Erie, CO 80516
303-444-3801

DBS Air Helicopter Services
P.O. Box 1770
Aspen, CO 81612
970-945-8808

SAILPLANES

Black Forest Soaring Society
24566 David C. Johnson Loop
Elbert, CO 80106
970-648-3063

The Cloud Base
5534 Independence Road
Boulder, CO 80301
303-530-2208

Gliders of Aspen
P.O. Box 175
Aspen, CO 81612
970-925-3694 (before 9:00 A.M.),
970-925-3418 (after 10:00 A.M.)

FIGHTERS

In the small category of airborne adventures, there is even a smaller subcategory of an excursion in authentic military training aircraft under the command of a veteran fighter pilot. This is sightseeing with a twist—a virtually real experience, rather than virtual reality, in the specialty of military flying.

Sky Fighters (based at Centennial Airport)
7395 South Peoria, Box C-11
Englewood, CO 80112
303-790-7375

PARAGLIDING

Small personal craft, motorized or not, provide airborne adventures that perhaps are the ultimate outdoor activity. Paragliding is a popular activity in the Alps that is just beginning to make its mark in the Colorado Rockies. Running a few steps, taking off from a hill or mountaintop with a parachute-like canopy above you, and riding the thermals is a matchless thrill. A paraglider weighs about ten pounds and folds down to backpack size. You can often take introductory lessons with a tandem paraglider, and further solo instruction involves radio contact between instructor and student. Ultralight flying is a bit like the motorized kin of paragliding. There's no running to take off in a craft that resembles a Wright Brothers plane powered by a small engine, and the hang time and distance covered are greater. As with paragliding, or *parapente* as it's known by Euro-speakers, ultralight trainers come in tandem models.

PARAGLIDING INSTRUCTION

Aspen Paragliding
P.O. Box 2432
417 South Spring Street
Aspen, CO 81612
970-925-7625

Parasoft Paragliding School
4445 Hastings Drive
Boulder, CO 80303
303-494-2820

ULTRALIGHT FLYING

Granby Sports Park
P.O. Box 771
64606 U.S. 40
Granby, CO 80446
970-887-2434

TIPS FOR PARAGLIDERS AND ULTRALIGHT FLYERS

What to Bring

Dressing for warmth in accordance with the season is similar to the "What to Bring" guidelines for aeronauts, except that you might not have to be prepared for the early-morning chill. In addition, paragliders need rugged protective clothing to prevent scrapes upon landing, and sturdy shoes that provide ankle support. A helmet and gloves, if not provided by the company, are also recommended.

What Not to Bring

Same advice regarding bulky objects as for hot-air ballooning.

13

MOTOWN MOVES

Roughly a hundred of Colorado's old mining roads, logging roads, unpaved pass roads, and even old railroad right-of-ways are ideal for four-wheel driving, which combines motorized thrills with great sightseeing. In many towns, especially in the southwestern central area (Leadville–Buena Vista area) and the southwestern area (Telluride-Ouray), 4WD rentals are available for self-driving tours.

Outfitters also offer guided four-wheel or jeep tours to picturesque old mining towns for those who prefer not to drive themselves. Sometimes they offer all-terrain vehicle (ATV) tours through the scenic backcountry, but the age limit is fourteen and older. The four-wheel season generally runs from May to October. Some areas are accessible to all types of vehicles, while others are restricted to motorcycles and ATVs. Many of the four-wheel-drive roads are subject to winter closures, but at that point, many of them, and

263

even some paved high-altitude roads that are not plowed in winter, are open for snowmobiling.

Organizations promoting motorized off-highway recreational travel and operating as information clearinghouses for these activities include:

Colorado Association of 4-Wheel-Drive Clubs
    (jeeps and other 4x4s)
P.O. Box 1413
Wheat Ridge, CO 80034
303-343-0646

Colorado Off Highway Vehicle Coalition
    (motorcycles and ATVs)
P.O. Box 620523
Littleton, CO 80162

Colorado Snowmobile Association
c/o Ann Burns, Corresponding Secretary
P.O. Box 474
South Fork, CO 81154
719-873-5724

INDEPENDENT OFF-HIGHWAY DRIVES

Old roads and railbeds may be suitable for jeeps and other 4x4 vehicles, ATVs, motorcycles, or some combination. Public managers issue recommendations or restrictions on such use. Several series of maps, guides, and video trail guides on the most popular roads and road systems are available from:

L&M Productions
2015 West Alameda Avenue
Denver, CO 80223
303-77-RIDER

FOUR-WHEEL-DRIVE AND ATV TOURS

Full-day trips generally include lunch. Because the vehicles are open, many outfitters also provide rain gear. For ATV rentals, helmets are also furnished.

OUTFITTERS, RIDES, AND OTHER DETAILS

Alpine Express 4-Wheel-Drive Tours
Gunnison County Airport
Gunnison, CO 81230
800-822-4844, 970-641-5074
Gunnison National Forest, including Paradise

Colorado West
332 Fifth Avenue
Ouray, CO 81427
800-648-JEEP, 970-325-4014
Yankee Boy Basin, Engineer Mountain; off roads to Telluride, Lake City, and Silverton

Crystal River 4x4 Tours
200 East State Street
Marble, CO 81623
970-963-1991
Crystal City, Lead King Basin, and marble-quarry tours in White River National Forest

Fun Time Jeep Tours
610 East U.S. 50
Salida, CO 81201
800-833-7238
Gold-mine and ghost-town tours; seasonal wildflower tours

Mad Adventures
P.O. Box 650
Winter Park, CO 80482
970-726-5290
4WD tours up Moffat Road to the Continental Divide; Arapaho National Forest

Nova Guides
P.O. Box 2018
Vail, CO 81658
970-949-4231
Jeep and ATV tours in White River National Forest, including historic Camp Hale area

River Runners
11150 U.S. 50
Salida, CO 81201
800-525-2081, 719-539-2144
Jeep tours to mines and ghost towns

San Juan Scenic Jeep Tours
P.O. Box 290W
480 Main Street
Ouray, CO 81427
970-325-4444
Yankee Boy Basin, Engineer Mountain, Lake City, Telluride via Black Bear and Imogene Pass, Silverton via Mystery Mountain Gold Mine

Steamboat Lake Outfitters
P.O. Box 749
Clark, CO 80428
970-879-4404, 970-879-5590
One- and two-hour and half-day ATV rides in Routt National
Forest; all-day and overnight options

Tiger Run Tours
P.O. Box 1418
Breckenridge, CO 80424
970-453-2231, 303-623-3032 (metro Denver)
4x4 ghost-town and gold-camp tours in Arapaho National
Forest

TOP SNOWMOBILING AREAS

Colorado boasts over 3,500 miles of marked snowmobile
trails, 2,000 of them groomed regularly (generally by local
snowmobile clubs). Frequently—and always in crowded
areas—snowmobilers, cross-country skiers, and snowshoers
use the same areas, but trail separation between motorized
and nonmotorized winter recreation works best.

The Colorado Snowmobile Association publishes maps
of fifteen popular snowmobile areas (Buena Vista–Taylor
Park, Carbondale–Grand Mesa, Colorado State Forest–
Roosevelt National Forest, Craig, Creede, Grand Lake,
Kremmling, Lake City, Leadville-Vail, Meeker, North Park,
Ophir Creek, Pagosa Springs, South Fork, and Steamboat
Springs). The Colorado Snowmobile Association also has
information on the Colorado Tour, an annual week-long
rally open to locals but really designed to give out-of-
staters an opportunity to ride their snowmobiles in an

organized event in the high country. In 1998, it is supposed to stretch to two weeks and cross the state lengthwise from New Mexico to Wyoming.

Colorado Snowmobile Association
c/o Evelyn Schittker, Recording Secretary
P.O. Box 1260
Grand Lake, CO 80447
970-627-8101

While many nonwilderness national forest areas and other public lands throughout the Colorado Rockies offer snowmobiling trails, several concentrations provide exceptional facilities for riders. These include not only trails but support services such as fuel sources, accommodations that cater to snowmobilers, and snowmobile dealers for parts and repairs.

AREAS, INFORMATION SOURCES, AND DETAILS

Grand Lake
Grand Lake Trail Groomers
P.O. Box 1247
Grand Lake, CO 80447
More than 150 miles of groomed trails in Arapaho National Forest; calls itself "the snowmobile capital of Colorado"

Lake City
c/o Lake City/Hinsdale County Chamber of Commerce
P.O. Box 430
Lake City, CO 81235
719-873-5512

More than 150 miles of groomed trails, many at 10,000–13,000 feet in elevation

South Fork Trailbusters Snowmobile Club
c/o The Inn Motel
P.O. Box 474
South Fork, CO 81154
800-223-9723, 719-873-5514
or
c/o Shirley Walker
29887 West U.S. 160
South Fork, CO 82254
719-873-5767
115 miles of groomed trails

SP Trail
c/o Glenwood Springs Chamber Resort Association
1102 Grand Avenue
Glenwood Springs, CO 81601
970-945-6589
155 miles between Glenwood Springs and Grand Junction; three lodges along the trail with food, fuel, and accommodations

SNOWMOBILE TOURS

Tours generally include the use of insulated, windproof snowsuits, gloves, and helmets. Some companies have outfitted their snowmobiles with heated handgrips and sometimes foot warmers, and tall windshields to protect riders from the wind and cold.

Colorado Outdoor Activity Guide

OUTFITTERS, RIDES, AND OTHER DETAILS

Action Adventures
P.O. Box 1786
Crested Butte, CO 81224
800-383-1974, 970-349-5909,
970-349-6598
One-hour ride; Gunnison National Forest; sunset dinner ride

Alpine Expeditions
P.O. Box 2259
Crested Butte, CO 81224
970-349-2441
One-hour introductory tour; two-hour tour to Gothic (old mining town); lunch tour to Chicken Bone Basin; dinner tours

Burt Rentals
P.O. Box 1268
Crested Butte, CO 81224
970-349-2441
Gunnison National Forest, Kebler Pass, Splains Gulch, Lake Irwin

Cottonwood Country Enterprises
P.O. Box 1648
215½ Tabor Street
Buena Vista, CO 81211
719-395-6727, 719-395-1098
One-hour and half- or full-day tours; Cottonwood Pass, Mineral Basin, Hancock, Tincup Pass; also snowcat tours

270

Glacier Mountain Adventures
8604 Glacier Road
St. Mary's Glacier
Idaho Springs, CO 80452
970-567-4322
Two-hour tours to scenic and mining areas

Good Times Tours
P.O. Box 68
Frisco, CO 80443
800-477-0144, 970-453-7604, 970-668-0930
12-, 15-, and 35-mile rides to the Continental Divide; Snow
Scoots

Nova Guides
P.O. Box 2018
Vail, CO 81658
970-949-4232
Hourly tours of Tigiwon Cabin, Arapaho National Forst;
half-day Camp Hale tours; snowcat tours

Piney River Ranch
Vail Associates
P.O. Box 7
Vail, CO 81657
970-476-3941
1.5-hour, half- and full-day, and twilight tours

Red Hot Ryders
480 Main Street
Ouray, CO 81427
800-325-4385, 970-325-4444

Rocky Mountain Sports
0412 Sun King Drive
Glenwood Springs, CO 81601
970-945-8885, 970-945-8498
SP Trail

SnoWest Snowmobile Rental & Tours
1642 Hummer Court
Leadville, CO 80461
719-486-1750
San Isabel National Forest; mine trips; guided and unguided
rides

Steamboat Lake Outfitters
P.O. Box 749
Clark, CO 80428
970-879-4404, 970-879-5590
One-hour, half-day, and full-day rides on over 100 miles of
trails

Tiger Run Tours
P.O. Box 1418
Breckenridge, CO 80424
970-453-2231, 303-623-3032 (metro Denver)
Ghost-town tours

Timberline Tours
P.O. Box 131
Vail, CO 81658
800-831-1414
White River National Forest

Trailblazer Snowmobile Tours
P.O. Box 3436
Winter Park, CO 80482
800-669-0134, 970-726-8452, 970-726-8032
Arapaho Natonal Forest; access to 120 miles of trails

White Mountain Snowmobile Tours
P.O. Box 980
Frisco, CO 80443
800-247-7238, 970-668-5323, 970-668-3572
One-, two-, and three-hour tours across the Continental
Divide, including views of the world's largest molybdenum
mine

FAMILY SNOWMOBILING

Youngsters must be at least fourteen years old to operate
their own snowmobiles, but children are permitted to ride
with adults. Some outfitters, such as Good Times Tours,
provide Snow Scoots, which are mini-snowmobiles, that
youngsters aged nine to fourteen can use for part of
the ride. Others, like Tiger Run Tours, supply free infant
carriers.

TRIPS FOR THE DISABLED

Because these activities involve riding rather than depending totally on motor skills, 4x4 or snowmobile tours provide access to the backcountry for many disabled people.

Tiger Run Tours is one company that promotes its services to wheelchair users and other disabled people.

TIPS FOR OFF-HIGHWAY RIDERS

Many roads through national forests, Bureau of Land Management lands, and other public lands are available for 4WDs and ATVs, but land managers ask that users respect the areas. Stay on dry roads, but try to avoid soft, dry conditions that quickly deteriorate roads. Resist the temptation to pioneer a new road or shortcut, and always travel around meadows, steep hillsides, stream banks, and lakeshores, which are easily damaged. Avoid driving over young trees, shrubs, and grasses beside designated roads. Obey gate closures and get permission to travel across private land. Respect and give the right-of-way to hikers, mountain bikers, and especially horseback riders, with whom motorized vehicles often share off-highway roads.

The U.S. Forest Service puts out a useful general-purpose handbook called *4-Wheeling*, which is available from the Lakewood regional office or from some district offices (see Appendix).

The *Colorado Trails Resource Guide* is a good source of information on trails for off-highway driving, as well as for hiking, mountain biking, and equestrian uses. Published for National Trails Day, it is available from:
Trail Mates of Colorado
10597 North Routt Lane
Westminster, CO 80221
303-465-1033

Tread Lightly is an important program that promotes education about low-impact four-wheeling. Information is available from:
Tread Lightly
P.O. Box 149
Ogden, UT 84402
800-966-9900

The Colorado Division of Parks & Recreation's (see Appendix) booklet called *Snowmobile Colorado* features information on regulations, snowmobile operation, and safe snowmobiling. The Colorado Snowmobile Association maintains a "snowline" number at 800-235-4480.

What to Bring

Outfitters generally supply all necessary protective gear, but you will want a hat and clothing that is appropriate for weather and for possible weather changes. (Remember such factors as wind chill and that when you are riding, you aren't generating the body heat that you would if you were hiking, biking, skiing, or snowshoeing.) If goggles are not provided, you should bring them. Also, remember the usual sunscreen, sunglasses, and other paraphernalia for outdoor activities in the high country.

HOW YOU CAN HELP

The Colorado Association of 4-Wheel-Drive Clubs (see above) and its component clubs around the state undertake

275

voluntary Adopt-a-Road maintenance, renovation, and clean-up projects on 4WD routes and support a four-wheel emergency-assistance program. CA4WDC also sponsors Bad to the Bone Future 4 Wheelers, an auxiliary for young people aged nine to fifteen who are introduced to off-highway activities in adult-supervised programs.

READING LIST

4x4 Trail Books is a series of regional map books for 4WD (CA4WDC, P.O. Box 1413, Wheat Ridge, CO 80334)

Snowmobile Colorado (Outdoor Empire Publishing, 511 Eastlake Avenue, Seattle, WA 98109)

APPENDIX

INFORMATION SOURCES

GENERAL TRAVEL INFORMATION BY REGION

Colorado disbanded its Tourism Board and abandoned its 800 number in 1993, making it more difficult to obtain information about activities and attractions. During the CTB's existence, the state was divided into six irregularly shaped regions, and, since its dissolution, various agencies are fulfilling general tourism-information requests. These regions are roughly as follows:

- Northwest Colorado (the Grand Lake side of Rocky Mountain National Park and Summit County in the east, Colorado National Monument and Grand Junction in the southwest, the corner bordering Utah and Wyoming in the northwest), 800-327-8789

- Southwest Colorado (Redstone, Crested Butte, and Gunnison in the north, Pagosa Springs in the southeast, and the Four Corners in the southwest), 800-933-4340
- South Central Colorado (Breckenridge and Copper Mountain in the north, Rush in the northeast, San Luis and Chama in the southeast, the New Mexico border on the south, and Creede in the southwest; includes Colorado Springs), 800-637-6238 (Note that at this writing, this number was not fulfilling requests but suggesting visitors contact local information sources.)
- North Central Colorado (the Estes Park side of Rocky Mountain National Park and Georgetown in the west, Fort Collins and the Wyoming border in the north, Larkspur and Palmer Lake in the south, and Strasburg and Byers in the east; includes Denver and Boulder), 800-444-0447
- Northeast Colorado (Carr and Rockport in the northwest, Julesburg in the northeast, Arapahoe and Cheyenne Wells in the southeast, and Kiowa and Elizabeth in the southwest), 800-544-8609
- Southeast Colorado (Pueblo in the northwest, Sheridan Lake and Towner in the northeast, Stonington and Campo in the southeast, Monument Park and Cuchara in the southwest, and Red Wing in the west), 800-338-6633

In late 1994, a commercial enterprise surfaced with the 800-COLORADO number that had been the Tourism Board's. Just what kind of information will be available from them was not clear as this book went to press, but it costs nothing to call them and find out.

COMPUTERIZED TRAVEL INFORMATION

The Colorado TravelBank started dispensing free travel and activities information in 1985, when the information superhighway was but a dirt road. Constantly updated information on attractions, sports, culture, dining, ski conditions, and a myriad of other details on places to go and things to do in Colorado are available to anyone with a computer and modem.

TravelBank Systems of Colorado
P.O. Box 371762
Denver, CO 80237
303-671-7669 (data), 303-745-8586 (voice)

FEDERAL AGENCIES

NATIONAL PARKS

National Park Service
P.O. Box 25287
Lakewood, CO 80203
303-969-2000

Mesa Verde National Park
Mesa Verde National Park, CO 81330
970-529-4465

Rocky Mountain National Park
Estes Park, CO 80517
970-586-1206

NATIONAL MONUMENTS

Black Canyon of the Gunnison National Monument
P.O. Box 1648
Montrose, CO 81401
970-249-7036

Colorado National Monument
Fruita, CO 81521
970-858-3617

Dinosaur National Monument
P.O. Box 210
Dinosaur, CO 81610
970-374-2216

Florissant Fossil Beds National Monument
P.O. Box 815
Florissant, CO 80816
719-748-3253

Great Sand Dunes National Monument
11500 State 150
Mosca, CO 81146
719-378-2312

Hovenweep National Monument
Mesa Verde National Park, CO 81330
970-529-4465

BUREAU OF LAND MANAGEMENT

2850 Youngsfield Street
Lakewood, CO 80215
303-239-3600

District Offices:
Cañon City
Craig
Grand Junction
Montrose

NATIONAL FORESTS

U.S. Forest Service, Rocky Mountain Region
11177 West Eighth Avenue
P.O. Box 25127
Lakewood, CO 80225
303-236-9431

NATIONAL FORESTS AND RANGER DISTRICTS
(AND LOCATIONS IF DIFFERENT)

Arapaho National Forest
240 West Prospect
Fort Collins, CO 80526
970-498-1722
Clear Creek (Idaho Springs)
Dillon (Silverthorne)
Middle Park (Kremmling)
Sulphur (Granby)

Grand Mesa National Forest
2250 U.S. 50
Delta, CO 81416
970-874-7691
Colbran
Grand Junction

Gunnison National Forest
2250 U.S. 50
Delta, CO 81416
970-874-7691
Cebolla (Gunnison)
Paonia
Taylor River (Gunnison)

Pike National Forest
1920 Valley Drive
Pueblo, CO 81008
719-545-8737
Pikes Peak (Colorado Springs)
South Park (Fairplay)
South Platte (Lakewood)

Rio Grande National Forest
1803 West Highway 160
Monte Vista, CO 81144
719-852-5941
Conejos Peak (La Jara)
Creede
Del Norte
Saguache

Roosevelt National Forest
140 West Prospect
Fort Collins, CO 80526
970-498-1100
Boulder
Estes/Poudre (Fort Collins)
Estes Park

Routt National Forest
29587 West U.S. 40, Suite 20
Steamboat Springs, CO 81625
970-879-1722
Bears Ear (Craig)
Hahns Peak (Steamboat Springs)
North Park (Walden)
Yampa

San Isabel National Forest
1920 Valley Drive
Pueblo, CO 81008
719-545-8737
Leadville
Salida
San Carlos (Cañon City)

San Juan National Forest
701 Camino del Rio
Durango, CO 81301
970-247-4874
Animas (Durango)
Dolores
Mancos
Pagosa Springs
Pine (Bayfield)

Uncompahgre National Forest
2550 U.S. 50
Delta, CO 81416
970-874-7691
Norwood
Ouray (Montrose)

White River National Forest
P.O. Box 948
Glenwood Springs, CO 81602
970-945-2521
Aspen
Blanco (Meeker)
Eagle
Holy Cross (Minturn)
Rifle
Sopris (Carbondale)

RECREATION AREAS

Brainard Lake Recreation Area
2995 Baseline Road, #110
Boulder, CO 80303
303-444-6600

Curecanti National Recreation Area
102 Elk Creek
Gunnison, CO 81230
970-641-2337

NATIONAL GRASSLANDS

Comanche National Grassland
27162 U.S. 287, Box 127
Springfield, CO 81073
719-523-6591

Pawnee National Grassland
660 O Street, #A
Greeley, CO 81703
970-353-5004

U.S. FISH AND WILDLIFE SERVICE

2850 Youngfield Street
Lakewood, CO 80215
303-259-3600

Field Offices—See Bureau of Land Management listing

STATE AGENCIES

Colorado State Parks and Recreation
1313 Sherman Street
Denver, CO 80203
303-866-3437

Colorado State Forest
Star Route, Box 91
Walden, CO 80480
970-723-8366

Colorado Division of Wildlife
6060 Broadway
Denver, CO 80203
303-297-1192

COLORADO WILDERNESS AREAS

Area	Acreage
American Flats	3,390
Big Blue	98,320
Bill Hare/Larson Creek	815
Black Canyon	11,180
Bowen Gulch	6,990
Buffalo Peaks	43,410
Byers Peak	8,095
Cache La Poudre	9,238
Collegiate Peaks	166,654
Comanche Peak	66,791
Davis Peaks	20,750
Eagles Nest	133,325
Flat Tops	235,035
Fossil Ridge	33,060
Great Sand Dunes	33,450
Greenhorn Mountain	22,040
Holy Cross	122,037
Hunter-Fryingpan	74,250
Indian Peaks	73,296
La Garita	103,986
Lizard Head	41,189
Lost Creek	118,790
Maroon Bells	181,138
Mesa Verde	8,100

Mount Evans	74,401
Mount Massive	30,540
Mount Sneffels	16,505
Mount Zirkel	139,818
Neota	9,924
Never Summer	13,702
Oh-Be-Joyful	5,500
Platte River	770
Piedra	62,550
Powderhorn	60,100
Ptarmigan Peak	13,175
Raggeds	59,159
Rahwah	73,020
Roubideau	19,650
Sangre de Cristos	226,455
Service Creek	47,140
South San Juan	158,790
Spruce Creek	8,330
Tabeguache	27,240
Vasquez Peak	12,300
West Needle/Weminuche	489,574
West Elk	176,092
Wheeler Addition	25,640

COLORADO FOURTEENERS

Peak	Elevation
Mt. Elbert	14,433 feet
Mt. Massive	14,421 feet
Mt. Harvard	14,420 feet
Blanca Peak	14,345 feet
La Plata Peak	14,336 feet

Uncompaghre Peak	14,309 feet
Crestone Peak	14,294 feet
Mt. Lincoln	14,286 feet
Grays Peak	14,270 feet
Mt. Antero	14,269 feet
Torreys Peak	14,267 feet
Castle Peak	14,265 feet
Quandary Peak	14,265 feet
Mt. Evans	14,264 feet
Longs Peak	14,255 feet
Mt. Wilson	14,246 feet
Mt. Shavano	14,229 feet
Mt. Princeton	14,197 feet
Mt. Belford	14,197 feet
Mt. Yale	14,196 feet
Crestone Needle	14,191 feet
Mt. Bross	14,172 feet
Kit Carson Peak	14,165 feet
El Diente Peak	14,159 feet
Maroon Peak	14,156 feet
Mt. Tabeguache	14,155 feet
Mt. Oxford	14,153 feet
Mt. Sneffels	14,150 feet
Mt. Democrat	14,148 feet
Capitol Peak	14,130 feet
Pikes Peak	14,110 feet
Snowmass Mountain	14,092 feet
Mt. Eolus	14,084 feet
Windom Peak	14,082 feet
Mt. Columbia	14,073 feet
Missouri Mountain	14,067 feet
Humboldt Peak	14,064 feet
Mt. Bierstadt	14,060 feet

Sunlight Peak	14,059 feet
Handies Peak	14,048 feet
Culebra Peak	14,047 feet
Ellingwood	14,042 feet
Mt. Lindsey	14,042 feet
Little Bear Peak	14,037 feet
Mt. Sherman	14,036 feet
Red Cloud Peak	14,034 feet
Pyramid Peak	14,018 feet
Wilson Peak	14,015 feet
Wetterhorn Peak	14,015 feet
North Maroon Peak	14,014 feet
San Luis Peak	14,014 feet
Huron Peak	14,005 feet
Mt. of the Holy Cross	14,005 feet
Sunshine Peak	14,001 feet

HOSTELS

Sometimes sleeping cheap seems to go well with outdoor activities, and for accommodations with a solid roof overhead, hostels can rarely be beaten.

Hostelling International/American Youth Hostels
Rocky Mountain Council
1310 College Avenue, Suite 315
Boulder, CO 80302
303-442-1166

COLORADO HOSTELS

Location	Name	Phone
Antonito	Conejos River AYH Hostel	719-376-2518
Breckenridge	Fireside Inn	970-453-6456

Colorado Springs	Garden of the Gods	719-475-9450
Denver	Melbourne Intl. AYH Hostel	303-292-6386
Estes Park	H-Bar-G Ranch Hostel	970-586-3688
Glenwood Springs	Glenwood Springs Hostel	970-945-8545
Grand Junction	Hotel Melrose	970-242-9636
Grand Lake	Shadowcliff Hostel	970-627-9220
Pitkin	Pitkin Hotel & Hostel	970-641-2725
Silverthorne	Alpine Hutte	970-468-6336
Winter Park	Winter Park Hostel	970-726-5356

OUTDOOR ACTIVITIES FOR THE DISABLED

In addition to specific programs and facilities indicated in individual chapters, the Colorado Division of Parks and Recreation has compiled an access guide to facilities and activities on federal and state lands that are accessible to the disabled. "Sightseeing" means that it is a scenic area for a drive-through visit or that there are some especially interesting special attractions. Most picnic areas and camping facilities have on-site drinking water. For details, contact the governing agency or request *Colorado on Wheels* from:
Colorado Commission on the Disabled
303 West Colfax Avenue
Denver, CO 80204
303-575-3056

SITES, FACILITIES, AND ACCESSIBLE ACTIVITIES

Front Range

Arapaho & Roosevelt National Forests
303-444-6001
Fishing, sightseeing

Barr Lake State Park
303-659-6005
Trails, sightseeing

Boyd Lake State Park
303-669-1739
Camping, picnic area, restrooms, showers

Chatfield State Park
303-791-7275
Trails, camping, fishing, picnic area, restrooms

Cherry Creek State Park
303-699-3860
Trails, camping, fishing, picnic area, restrooms

Golden Gate State Park
303-592-1502
Trails, camping, fishing, picnic area, restrooms, sightseeing

Pike National Forest
719-636-1602
Braille trail, trails, camping, fishing, picnic area, restrooms

San Isabel National Forest
719-545-8737
Trails, camping, fishing, picnic area, camping, restrooms, showers, sightseeing

Rocky Mountain National Park
970-586-2371
Trails, camping, fishing, picnic area, restrooms, showers, sightseeing

Roxborough State Park
303-973-3959
Sightseeing, restrooms

Northwest

Colorado State Forest
970-723-8366
Trails, camping, fishing, picnic area, restrooms, sightseeing

Fish Creek Falls Recreation Area
970-879-1870
Trails, picnic area, restrooms, sightseeing

Highline State Recreation Area
970-858-7208
Fishing, picnic area, restrooms, sightseeing

Island Acres State Recreation Area
970-464-0548
Camping, picnic area, fishing

Rifle Gap State Recreation Area
970-625-1607
Camping, restrooms, sightseeing

Routt National Forest
970-879-1722
Camping, picnic area, restrooms, sightseeing

Stagecoach Reservoir State Recreation Area
970-736-2436
Camping, restrooms, sightseeing

Vega State Recreation Area
970-487-3407
Camping, fishing, picnic area, restrooms, sightseeing

White River National Forest
970-945-2521
Camping, picnic areas, restrooms, fishing, sightseeing

Southwest

Crawford State Recreation Area
970-921-5721
Trails, restrooms, sightseeing

Gunnison National Forest
970-527-4131
Campground, picnic areas, restrooms, sightseeing

Ridgway State Recreation Area
970-626-5822
Camping, picnic area, restrooms, sightseeing

Trinidad State Recreation Area
719-846-6951
Camping, fishing, picnic area, restrooms, sightseeing

Plains

Bonny State Recreation Area
970-354-7306
Camping, fishing, restrooms, showers, sightseeing

Lathrop State Park
719-738-2376
Camping, picnic area, fishing, restrooms, showers, sight-seeing

Pueblo State Recreation Area
719-561-9320
Trails, camping, picnic area, fishing, restrooms, showers, sightseeing

READING LIST, CONT.

Books by Mail

Topographic maps are available at hiking, outdoor, and specialized map stores or from:
U.S. Geological Survey
P.O. Box 25046
Denver Federal Center
Denver, CO 80225
303-236-5829

Guidebooks and maps for cyclists, hikers, and back-packers are available from:
Colorado Trails Books and Maps
12272 West 32nd Avenue
Wheat Ridge, CO 80033
303-232-8243

Guidebooks for rafters and kayakers, historical books on early exploration of Colorado's rivers, videos, and maps are available from:

Westwater Books
P.O. Box 2560
Evergreen, CO
800-628-1326, 303-674-5410

Books on technical climbing, expeditions, and mountaineering, both current and historical, are available from:
Chessler Books
26030 Highway 74, Box 399
Kittredge, CO 80457
800-645-8502, 303-670-0093

Books on cycling are available from:
VeloNews
1830 North 55th Street
Boulder, CO 80301
800-234-8356, Ext. 6

INDEX

296

299

301

303

304

305

Colorado Outdoor Activity Guide

309

Other titles in the Outdoor Activity Guide series:

Connecticut Outdoor Activity Guide
Georgia Outdoor Activity Guide
Pennsylvania Outdoor Activity Guide
Virginia Outdoor Activity Guide
Washington Outdoor Activity Guide

All books are $9.95 at bookstores.
Or order directly from the publisher (add $3.00 shipping
and handling for direct orders):

Country Roads Press
P.O. Box 286
Castine, Maine 04421
Toll-free phone number: **800-729-9179**